Water Break Its Neck

Frederick Grice

Water Break
Its Neck

Oxford University Press

Oxford Toronto Melbourne

Oxford University Press, Walton Street, Oxford OX2 6DP

Oxford New York Toronto
Delhi Bombay Calcutta Madras Karachi
Petaling Jaya Singapore Hong Kong Tokyo
Nairobi Dar es Salaam Cape Town
Melbourne Auckland

and associated companies in
Beirut Berlin Ibadan Nicosia

Oxford is a trade mark of Oxford University Press

British Library Cataloguing in Publication Data

Grice, Frederick
Water break its neck.
I. Title
823'.914 [J] PZ7

ISBN 0-19-271535-6

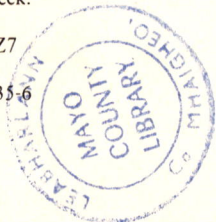

TO LAURA AND LUKE

Typeset by Leaper & Gard Ltd, Bristol, England
Printed in Great Britain by
Biddles Ltd., Guildford

Chapter 1

Cefn

When my uncle was alive — I call him my uncle but he was really my great-uncle — I went for some time to a school in Builth kept by an old man who told us that when he was a young man he was a soldier in the Peninsular War against Napoleon. I went there because my aunt wanted me to learn to read and write. She was a good reader herself and had books in her house — a rare thing for a shepherd's wife in our part of the world — I think she taught me more than the old soldier at Builth. But as soon as I had learnt to read and write and had mastered simple arithmetic, I left to help my uncle. He was growing old, and walking the Fron was getting too much for him.

I think my old schoolmaster was pleased to see the back of me, for he never forgave me for a trick I played on him. One day he showed us his Victoria medal, of which he was very proud, and when his back was turned I pocketed it, and we pretended that he had mislaid it. We arranged for him to find it in the end, but he always suspected that I was the one behind the hoax and never trusted me from then on.

I got myself into trouble on a second occasion when I played truant with a boy from Builth called Glyn. We went fishing in a stretch of the water that we knew was dangerous, because there was a notice warning everybody that there were deep holes and whirlpools in the river. Glyn vexed me by snatching at my rod when I'd hooked a fish. I don't know what came over me but I pushed him into the water and he fell into one of the holes. I managed to get him out but he must have had a fright because he would never come down to the river with me again.

I didn't mind leaving school. I preferred being on the

1

Fron, helping with the lambing, burning off the heather — even digging drains, though that was the dullest of all my tasks. When my uncle died, I told my aunt that I would look after her and the flock. I really don't know what I meant when I said I would look after her, but I knew what I meant when I said I would see to the flock. I was only thirteen but already I knew a lot about shepherding.

Ours wasn't a large flock, but we had plenty of land, and I had dreams of having one day the biggest flock in Radnorshire. As soon as I could, I meant to get my aunt to buy me a brand new hut like the one that Richard of Nant Bran had got himself. My only shelter in bad weather was a cave. Matty the Mole had shown it to me and it lay on the far side of the Fron. It wasn't as convenient as Richard's new hut, but it was mine and nobody ever disputed it with me. I sometimes slept there at lambing time, and I kept kindling and food there. It was called Llewellyn's Cave, and Matty the Mole once told me that the Welsh Prince had slept there on the eve of a great battle against the English.

Talybont where I lived was a small village tucked away under the edge of Radnor Forest. There were not many houses, and they were mostly huddled together around the church and the Swan. The Swan was nothing much more than a pothouse, but it was busy enough, and that was more than you could say about the church. Mr Williams, who was the Rector of Corris as well as the Vicar of Talybont, was a quarrelsome man, more interested in squabbling and even fighting with his parishioners than showing them a good example. There was a woman in Corris who kept some whiskers in a box and she said she had pulled them out of Mr Williams's beard during a fight. He often appeared in the pulpit with black eyes and bruises all over his face, and instead of a sermon he would boast how he got the better of some bruiser or other. His favourite saying was, "Don't do what I do. Do what I tell you to do." He came to Talybont for special occasions, weddings and funerals, and Holy Communion at Easter and Christmas. In between whiles nobody went to church. The Methodists had a little Chapel of their own.

2

My aunt told me that in the village where they had lived before coming to Talybont they had had lantern lectures and concerts and penny readings, but there was nothing like this in Talybont.

Cefn, my aunt's house, was one of the biggest in the village. There was no upstairs, but we were not short of rooms. There was a stone over the doorway with

L   S

P

1752

carved on it. The initials stood for Llewellyn and Susannah Phillips, her grandfather and grandmother, who had built the house for themselves after their wedding in Builth. He had discovered some medicinal springs somewhere, maybe in Builth itself, but he had made no money out of them, and had taken up shepherding at Cefn. It was a bit of a come-down for a clever man, but he had stuck to it and stayed at Cefn for the rest of his life. There must not have been any grandsons because the house came to my aunt.

It was about a year after the death of my uncle that she told me these things.

"Gareth," she said, "I want you to know that Cefn is mine and nobody else's. The cow is mine as well, and the flock of Beulahs and the grazing rights on the Fron, and when I go I want them to pass to you and nobody but you."

"You don't want to talk like that, aunt. You're still young. You have a long time to live yet."

"No, I'm not as strong as I was Gareth. I've had one or two signs lately. I won't last much longer. So I want you to have a look at this."

"What is it?"

"It's my last will and testament. It's all done properly, with witnesses. I've put down that everything is to be yours when I pass on. There's just one thing I'm worried about. Mr Bevan and his wife were the witnesses but they've gone to Australia since then. I should get it done again but some-how I haven't the heart to start all over again."

3

"What will Jago think about the will? What will he do when he gets to know?"

"I'll tell you what he'll do. He'll try to get Cefn from you. He'll try to claim it. You'll have to fight him."

"But he's a man. I can't fight him."

"I don't mean with fists. With the will. That's why I'm going to give it to you now. Keep it safe, Gareth, and when it comes to the push, face him with it."

"I haven't anywhere to keep it safe."

"I've thought of that. I'm going to put it in my little writing desk. You'll find it wrapped in a piece of oilskin — that's to keep it dry if ever you want to take it out — and here's the key for the desk."

"Where do I keep it?"

"Tie it round your neck. I've put it on this little chain. Hang it round your neck and don't take it off."

"I don't like to hear you talk like this, aunt."

"I've finished now. We'll leave the key on my ring till it's needed. Just read to me a little bit afore I go to bed."

Ever since I could remember I had read to my aunt before she went to bed. She started the habit to make sure I could read, and continued it because she liked to be read to. I knew what she would like. She had an old book about an old Bishop of Hereford who was supposed to have made a journey to the moon. She never tired of hearing it and I never tired of reading it to her.

Chapter 2

The Wild Rover

My aunt always went to bed early. She believed that I did
the same, but I didn't. I didn't need as much sleep as she did.
So as soon as my aunt had put out her candle I would go
down to the Swan to see what was happening there. I wasn't
allowed to go inside, Mrs Priddy wouldn't have that, but I
used to meet Evan Lloyd or Edwin Pugh there and we would
sit in the darkness just outside the door, watching everybody
who went in and came out, and listening to the quarrelling
and shouting that was going on inside.

One night, after a big auction of sheep at a farm not far
away, I slipped out as soon as my aunt had gone to sleep and
went down to the Swan. I found Evan waiting for me. We
took our usual place just outside the door. The men came in
in twos and threes. A lot of money must have changed hands
at the auction and they were coming to celebrate their
bargains. We watched them go in and heard the noise rising
as they grew more and more drunk and quarrelsome. Then
when it looked as if everybody who was going to come had
already arrived, we saw a stranger coming towards us out of
the darkness.

He was a big man, with broad shoulders and long swing-
ing arms, and he loomed out of the darkness into the stream
of light that fell through the open door, like a giant. In his
thick ragged clothes, made even bulkier by the rents and
tears in them, his lofty battered hat and vast shabby boots,
he was like some creature from my aunt's book. He paused
for a moment, drew himself up to his full height, and then
passed through the open door.

Two or three men who had started up a long unintelligible
Welsh song went on singing in their high piercing voices,

and from time to time even *their* noise was drowned by the sound of quarrelling. But after a while then the men stopped singing and the quarrelling subsided. I heard someone say, "Give a little order now, and we'll have a song from the stranger!" and out of the silence that followed there arose a single voice, more deep and powerful than any I had ever heard. Evan and I piled a few stones under the only window of the Swan, climbed on them and pressed our faces against the cold smoky pane. Through the dirty pane and the fog of tobacco smoke that rose from the men's pipes I could see the stranger, standing head and shoulders above the drovers and shepherds. Matty was there in a far corner with his eyes turned admiringly on him. I had never heard the song before, but I heard it so many times in the days that followed that I never forgot the words.

I've been a wild rover for many a year,
And I've spent all my money on whiskey and beer.
But now I'll give over, put money in store,
And I'll be a wild rover no never no more.
    And it's no, nay, never, no nay, never no more,
    I'll be a wild rover, no never no more.

I went into an alehouse I'd often frequent,
And I told the landlady my money was spent.
I asked for some credit and she answered me, "Nay,
Such custom as yours I can get any day."

Then out of my pocket I drew silver and gold,
And the landlady's eyes, they began for to roll.
She said, "We've got spirits and beers in galore,
So drink up my lads as you've ne'er drunk before."

I'll go home to my parents and tell what I've done,
And I'll ask them to pardon the prodigal son,
And if they'll accept me, as they've done before,
Then I'll play the wild rover no never no more.
    And it's no, nay, never, no nay, never no more,
    I'll be a wild rover, no never no more.

When he had finished, the men started cheering and clapping him on the back, and I saw them pushing cans of beer towards him. The Welsh drovers loved a good singer and would do anything for him. Evan and I stood jostling on the stones, but somebody saw us, and Mrs Priddy came out and told us to clear off.

We sat beside the door waiting for the stranger to sing again, but somebody started on 'Ar Hyd Y Nos', and after that it was impossible to tell who was singing and who was not. Then a man came lurching out through the door and staggered away into the darkness. We heard him fall down on the roadside and lie there cursing and vomiting. We did not go to him. It was common for the men to lie down by the roadside and sleep off their drink. Then some time later the stranger came out, looked round and walked away into the darkness from which he had appeared. It was hard to see what happened but I thought I could see him half-stumble over the drunken man, then bend down and turn him over, maybe to see if he was injured or ill, then push him over with his foot and walk away.

It was time for us to go as well. I went off following the stranger who had walked towards Cefn, but he must have turned off at some point because I lost him and didn't see him again.

But I saw somebody else.

There was someone leaning over the wall looking down on Cefn. I caught sight of him outlined against the pale grey sky. It was impossible to mistake him. Only one man spied upon us in this way — Jago, my aunt's nephew, and the one man I was ashamed to have to call a relative. As soon as he saw he was observed he ducked behind the wall and made off, but I had seen him, and not for the first time, spying greedily on the house that he coveted.

7

Chapter 3

The Waterfall

1872 was one of the worst lambing years that anybody could remember. We had heavy falls of snow just after Christmas, and then week after week of rain. I did my best to get the ewes into some kind of shelter during the worst of the weather, but they didn't like being herded at that time of the year. They liked to go off and drop their lambs by themselves. The lambs had come and had stood up to the weather better than I thought they would, but with the streams full and the mawn bogs deep with treacherous pools both ewes and lambs were in danger of being stranded or drowned. I went up the Fron as often as I could, hauling the sodden ewes out of gullies and hooking lambs back on to drier ground, but I was always worried about the ones I'd missed.

However the ground began to dry out at last and I got round the flock for the first time for days. We hadn't lost too many, and the ones we had lost were beyond saving. I went round flinging the dead lambs up on to the top of the thorn-bushes. We didn't like to leave them where the dogs could get at them. Then I thought I'd go and see how much water was going over the waterfall.

We didn't speak Welsh at Cefn — my aunt thought of herself and me as English, though we were on the Welsh side of the border, and she didn't like me to use Welsh words — but most of the shepherds knew Welsh and nearly every farm and village had a Welsh name: Skirrid, Nant Melan, Wern y Pentre, Llanfihangel, Beulah. Only the waterfall had an English name: Water Break Its Neck.

This was the place where the Dulas left the moor and plunged into the ravine. It began its descent with a series of short leaps, dropping to a first ledge, then a second and a third: then it suddenly pitched over the lip of the fall, plummeting in a sheer drop of forty feet into a black pool.

I had never got nearer to that pool than the lip of the fall. I didn't know anyone who had got down to it, who knew how deep it was, and what kind of currents there were under the surface. It was shut in by walls of black rock, as smooth as glass, with no crack in them. There may have been some way down but I never found it.

Between the waterfall and the lower ground where the Dulas reappeared and went on to join the Wye, there was a ravine of tumbled rocks and fallen tree trunks and other obstacles that I'd heard the men talk about but had never seen. Once or twice I had started up-river, hoping to get to the pool that way, but I had never got very far. Nor had I ever got anybody to go with me. None of the older shepherds could see the point of spending time in a place where the only sheep you could see were dead ones, and the younger ones were a bit afraid of it.

As I stood on the lip of the fall looking down for the hundredth time into those black and secret waters I saw that something had found its way there. Circling slowly in the whirlpool was the white and swollen shape of a lamb. I knew its story. No doubt it had fallen into the Dulas, been washed down from ledge to ledge and pitched into the pool like a sailor who had died at sea. For a moment I watched it rotating like a pale planet around the vortex of the pool, brushing its way through the flimsy galaxy of fawn-coloured foam. It was doubly beyond me. It was dead; and it had fallen into the inaccessible whirlpool of Water Break Its Neck.

It was quiet up on the Fron, but more people crossed it than you would think, and hardly a week passed without my seeing Matty the Mole on his way to the fields down by Risca. He made his living catching moles, curing their skins and selling them to be made up into trousers. He told me that the navvies that were working on the railways liked nothing better than a pair of moleskin trousers. There were not many moles on the Fron but there were plenty down in the pastures and orchards around Risca.

Matty was a short sparely-built old man with a sharp little

face that he cocked as he talked like a banty cockerel looking for something to peck at. He was dressed in a dark grey coat and knickerbockers, and an old deer-stalker with the flaps tied on top with a frayed ribbon like a cock's comb. All his movements were impatient and quick. When he walked he almost broke into a run, and on horseback he dug in his heels and flapped his arms as if he was in a race. A blind man would always know when Matty was around. He had a kind of salve that he made up himself to attract ants, and the smell seemed to have got not only into his clothes but under his skin. Even his pony smelt of it.

"How you been getting on in this terrible weather, Gareth?" he said one day. "Lost a lot of lambs, have you?"

"A few."

"Gone over Break Its Neck, eh?"

"Yes."

"It's a terrible deep hole at the bottom of that waterfall. Nobody bottomed that place yet."

"Has anybody tried?"

"I was there when two or three fellers from Risca had a go. Do you know what they did?"

"No."

"They got the bell ropes out of the church and tied them together, and then they tied a hundred pound weight at the end of the ropes, and then they let it down."

"Did they bottom it?"

"Bottom it? They never got nowhere near the bottom, man. I tell you, nobody's ever found out how deep that place is. There's been some queer stories told about it one time and another. You know that big green tump, just at the top?"

"Yes."

"Well, there was a robber once and he used to have a castle on the top of that tump. And he used to capture men and women and children as well, and if nobody would pay a ransom for them, do you know what he did?"

"No."

"He used to get hold of them and throw them down into the pool. By God, he must have been a bloodthirsty old ruffian, mustn't he? How you getting on with that uncle of yours these days?"

"Jago?"

"Yes. How's he making out now he lives on his own?"

"I don't know. And I don't care."

"You don't sound as if you had much time for him."

"I haven't. I don't like him."

"What you got against him?"

"He's greedy. And he's sly."

"Oh he's no worse than a lot of folks in this place. He hasn't got as bad a name as all that. You don't want to get a down on him just because he's done one or two queer things. There's a lot of goodness in him, don't forget that."

Matty always made me uneasy when he spoke like this. Whenever anyone began to speak of Jago I began to get uneasy. The truth was that I was afraid of him in a way that I could hardly understand.

All my life I had been afraid of him. I had never been inside his house, and my aunt had never dreamt of visiting him, but I can remember when I was younger, dreadful noises coming from it, sounds that could be heard all over the village. The boys said it was Jago's sister, the madwoman, who was having one of her fits, and when I asked my aunt about it, she said, yes, Jago had a sister who was mad, and she ought to have been taken to the asylum at Hereford long ago, but Jago wouldn't let her go. She spoke as if Jago was to blame, but many of the women in Talybont said that he had done the right thing, and that if his sister had gone to the asylum that would have been the end for her. All I knew was that the noises that came from the house terrified and fascinated us, and we used to hang around because somebody had said that she would run out with no clothes on if she got the chance. I think I first began to be afraid of Jago because I thought that he might turn like his sister, and suddenly lose his senses as she had done.

Everybody knew that he was a violent man. Once he was up before the magistrates for assaulting a gypsy outside the Swan and nearly kicking him to death, and if he had not pleaded that he had to look after his sister, and didn't know

11

what would happen to her if he went to jail, he would have been given a stiff sentence. He wasn't the only violent man in Talybont, and fights were two a penny, especially after the sheep sales at Builth, or when the Welsh cattle drovers turned up on their way to Hereford. But there was something about him that disturbed me and made me lose my head at times. I felt that he could easily get to the point where he would not know what he was doing, and at times like that he would not stop short of murder to get his own way.

"I don't know," went on Matty, and with every word I became more and more uneasy, "why it is you and your aunt can't get on better with Jago. After all, you're as alike as two peas, you and him. He's more like your brother than your uncle."

This was not the first time that Matty had mentioned how much I looked like Jago. I hated him to remind me of it partly because I could not bear to be classed with my so-called uncle, and partly because I knew it was true. There was a resemblance and I hated myself because of it.

That night when my aunt had gone to bed I looked at myself once more in the glass, and saw once more there the coarse reddish hair that grew straight down from the crown over the ears and the brow and would not be brushed back, the thin nose and the cleft chin that Jago had. I would have cut my hair as short as a convict's if I could have found the scissors. Instead I plastered some macassar oil on it and tried to part it in a new way — an unsuccessful move because the next morning my aunt was horrified at the state of the pillow and made me wash the oil out of my hair. After that I gave up trying to change my looks, and took to trying to hold myself in a different way so that I should be as unlike Jago as I could. He held himself slackly, so I tried to cultivate a military bearing, and no doubt made myself look ridiculous and pretentious.

Chapter 4

Jago

Summer was very slow in coming that year. It was colder in May than it was in December, and colder in June than it was in May. All the trees in the valley looked in bad shape. The cold weather had killed many of them, and whatever blossom came on the fruit trees was blown off before it could set properly. We began to wonder if the summer would ever come. All the shepherds lost lambs, and we suffered, if anything, more than most. The strange thing was that most of the ewes twinned in the end, so that we didn't lose too badly, but it was a miserable season for shepherding, and on many a day I had to seek refuge in the cave.

But warmer weather came in the end. Towards the end of June the air grew warmer, even oppressive. I used to wake in the night hearing my aunt getting up to open the windows in her room. She suffered in thundery weather, and couldn't breathe properly on sultry nights.

Although it was early when I went out, the men were at work in the village. A team of horses was struggling up the slope with a huge load of timber. The carter had got down and was holding the leader by the bit trying to keep the team moving. The flanks of the horses were already dark with sweat, and I could see the perspiration running off the man's face. A gang of boys had got behind the load and were trying to push, but the carter swore at them and told them to clear off.

The road from Cefn up the Fron was known as Green Lane, and halfway up there was a copse where I sometimes sheltered if I was caught by bad weather, and in the copse there was a tree that I always stopped to look at. Many of the people of Talybont had odd habits. If my aunt had gone out of the house and then remembered something she had left behind, she would always sit down again for a few moments before she went out again. Then there was a boy who went to school with me at Builth who wouldn't go into the classroom before he had touched every railing on the wall outside the old soldier's house. My peculiar habit was to take a look at my tree.

It was an ash, thick at the bole but thinning away until the trunk narrowed like a waist. Then it thickened again at the shoulders and divided into two branches that reached upward like arms, and at the division, just where the arms began, there was a hole, as if a head had been struck off. With its waisted body and lifted arms it looked like a headless crucifix, but in another light, especially in the dusk, it would look like a beast that was leaning forward to clutch me. At times I felt a kind of pity for it, but at others it looked ugly and menacing.

That morning I was glad to get up on the Fron. It was cooler there, but the flies were coming off the bracken and I was glad of my big-brimmed hat. As I went round the flock Bryn followed me, panting. Whenever I gave him a breather he lay down with his paws stretched in front of him, his great tongue lolling out of his mouth.

I finished my round about midday and sat down with my back up against a flat rock that I liked to rest against. I was thinking of going over to the far side of the hill to look at the cave when I saw Jago coming towards me. I knew that he was looking for me. He never came up the Fron unless he had to.

I did not speak to him. He wiped his neck with a dirty rag that he took from his pocket, trying to drive away the flies that swarmed round him.

"Are these all our Susannah's?" he said looking round the flock.

"Yes," I replied. I hated to hear him speak of my aunt in this way.

"She's got a tidy flock. How many ewes and lambs do you reckon she has?"

"About three hundred, I think."

14

"You're not very sure, are you? What's the matter, haven't you counted them?"

"I think I know how many there are."

"Why don't you give me a straight answer, then?"

"I didn't know you wanted the exact figure."

"You seen that dead lamb down by the Dulas?"

"Yes."

"You don't seem to mind much about it, do you?"

"I couldn't save it. It was weak when it was born. I couldn't do anything for it."

"You don't seem to have made much of an effort, have you?"

I did not reply. I wanted to ask him what right he had to question me like this, but I didn't want to rile him. He was a dangerous man.

"How many of these will you be taking to Builth this year?"

"About a hundred."

"You'll make a fair bit out of them, won' you?"

Again I did not reply.

"Susannah should make a good profit out of them. How much do you think she'll get?"

"I don't know. It's not my business."

"What sort of a shepherd do you call yourself? Don't you know what price to get for a lamb?"

"I'll take what they fetch."

"And get swindled, most likely. You've lost a fair number of lambs this year, I've heard."

"Everybody has. It's been a bad year."

"I've heard that excuse before. What about that dog of yours? Is he any good? He looks a poor specimen to me. What's the matter with him?"

"He doesn't like strangers."

"You mean he doesn't like me, don' you?"

I didn't reply. I wanted to but I was never sure what Jago would do, and when that wild violent look came over him I thought of his sister and was afraid that he too might suddenly take leave of his senses.

"Well, I don't like him," he went on. "I think he's a bad 'un, and if he was mine it wouldn't take me long to get rid of

15

him. He'd soon be in that pool there with a big stone round his neck."

"Then it's a good job you'll never get him," I muttered.

"What's that you said?"

"Nothing."

"You're a cheeky young sod, aren't you? But you'll get the cheek knocked out o' you afore long."

I thought he was going to strike me. I think he would have had a go at me if it hadn't been for Bryn, but he turned away with a sneering look on his face, and went off. He had come without a hat, and the flies were around his head in a cloud. I watched him shambling off, waving his hands to stop them from settling on his straight red hair. I hated him and was ashamed to think that I was related to him. And I knew he was no shepherd. He didn't know the flock and he didn't know the Fron, and though he had lived in Talybont all his life I had an idea that he had never found his way to my cave.

Chapter 5

Disasters

It was about this time that two events occurred that had serious consequences for me.

The first was an accident of which I was only a spectator, but for which I came in for a great deal of unfair blame, and it happened to Evan Lloyd, the boy who was with me when I heard the stranger singing in the Swan. I thought he was my friend, but after what happened I changed my mind.

We didn't have proper drainage in Talybont, and every big house had to do with a cesspool. The Swan had one of the biggest, and, like all cesspools, every now and then it had to be cleaned out. It was a dirty job and the men usually did it in the hours of darkness. On this occasion they drained it and shot the contents into a big hole they had dug at the bottom of the garden. I think they meant to fill it in the following day.

Unluckily the night after they had tipped the contents of the cesspool into the pit was very windy, and the high wind brought down a great quantity of cherries from the big morella that grew close to the pit. When I was walking past with Evan he saw some cherries resting on the apparently firm surface of the pit — the refuse had dried in the high wind and looked solid — and he was so greedy for them that before I could stop him he had jumped down, never thinking that the stuff would give way under him. He began to sink immediately, and the more he struggled the deeper he sank. I leant over and tried to pull him out, but I could make no headway and was afraid that he would pull me in after him. I thought for a moment that he would go under and drown in front of my eyes. So I left him and ran for help, and by good luck I met a man who was taking a horse to be shod.

17

When we came to the pit Evan was nearly under, but I noticed that he still had a bunch of cherries in his hand. The man, who was a stranger, got Evan first of all to hold on to a big stick that he reached down to him, then threw him a rope and told him to twist it round him and tie under his arms. Then he pulled him out, covered with slime and smelling like a midden. Evan got rid of the dirt and smell by dipping himself in the brook, but he had to go home with wet clothes. He was afraid of his father who was a very violent man and never thought twice of using his belt on his family, so he tried to excuse himself by saying that he wasn't to blame and that I'd pushed him in. In a few hours it was all over the village that I had had a fight with Evan and tried to kill him.

I never thought that the people of Talybont would have believed such a story, but in the next few days I learnt that they were far more ready to suspect my aunt and me than to trust us. I never thought they would turn against us so suddenly, but they did.

I can see now that I was having to pay for my aunt's strange ways. She had lived in Talybont for many years, but she had never mixed with the women and there was nobody you could have called her close friend. Both she and her husband had kept themselves very much to themselves, as people very often do who feel that their family has come down in the world. The women respected her, but she never welcomed them in her house, and they thought her secretive and stand-offish. I must have come in for some of the mistrust they felt towards her, because I began to get cold looks from everybody, and I learnt, to my vexation, that they were all more willing to believe Evan's story than mine.

I daresay the truth would have come out in the end, but all this could not have happened at a worse time for me. Towards the end of July the second serious event occurred. My aunt died suddenly, and her death, coming as it did when I was under a cloud, turned out to be a disaster.

18

Chapter 6

Flight

My aunt died on the last day of July. She died while I was up on the Fron. When I came home that evening I was met by a woman whom I had not seen before, and who told me to keep away till my aunt had been properly laid out. When at last I was allowed in I found the house filled with a strange sweet smell. The blinds and curtains were all drawn.

Mrs Griffiths — she told me her name — said that she had made a promise to my aunt a long time ago that she would lay her out and see to the funeral. She told me she lived at the other side of the Wern Mountain and never left her house except to lay out her friends. Maybe that was why I had never seen her before. She was very kind and very quiet, but I didn't know what to do. I felt that I was a stranger in the house. Mrs Griffiths didn't say much to me, but I gathered that I was to sleep in the kitchen or in the stable till the funeral was over. My aunt had been laid out in her own bedroom, and Mrs Griffiths had taken mine. I chose the stable. I couldn't bear the silence of the house. It was far better hearing the cow pulling at the hay and jangling her chain than lying in the kitchen in that terrible silence.

Between my aunt's death and her funeral I spent all day on the Fron, wondering what would happen when the service was over and Mrs Griffiths had gone back home.

There were not many mourners at the funeral. We had no relations in Talybont, or anywhere else for that matter, except Jago. I saw Matty in the church (and smelt him too) and, to my surprise, Mrs Priddy from the Swan.

"I'm sorry to see your aunt go, Gareth," said Matty when we were coming away from the graveyard. "She was a good woman, but I seen her failing for the last few months. And

19

last Thursday when I was riding over from Builth and heard the soul bell I said to myself, 'That's for Susannah Phillips for a certainty.'"

"Yes, it was Thursday when she died."

"You'll be on your own now, Gareth. Have you told the bees yet?"

"Not yet."

"Well you'd better hurry up and tell them that your aunt has died now. I knew a man at Builth once that didn't believe what I told him about the bees, and a week after his father died all the bees swarmed on him and blow me if he could get one of them back. Well, funeral or no funeral, Gareth, we got to earn a living. Don't forget now, tell them bees your mistress has died and if ever you see a mole coming up in your garden, just you send for me."

Mrs Griffiths left Cefn the day after the funeral. I couldn't bear being in the house without my aunt. There was some food left over from the funeral meal, so I packed some in my bag and went off to the Fron. I stayed up there all day.

When I came back that night I was surprised to see the door standing open. I thought that Mrs Griffiths must have forgotten something and come back for it, but I knew that it wasn't like her to leave doors open. I made Bryn sit down behind the wall and went quietly up to a window.

It wasn't Mrs Griffiths who was in the house. It was Jago. He was searching for something. I saw him opening drawers and cupboards, unhooking the pictures from the walls and looking behind them, throwing back the mats on the floor and pulling the cloth from the table. He was working very methodically, putting everything back in its place. When he came to the little writing desk, he tried to open it with his pocket knife. When he couldn't get it open he stood looking at it for a while as if he meant to steal it, but he seemed to decide against it. He stood for a while scratching the top of his head with his finger nail. Then he put the desk down and went into the kitchen. I went back for Bryn and we hid behind the wall till Jago came out.

I knew what he was after, and I knew he would come back

for it. I opened the desk, took out the will in its oilskin cover and stitched it into my belt. I did not know whether that was sensible or not but that was the best place I could think of.

I left the key around my neck. There wasn't much point now that I had removed the will, but I didn't think of that and in the end it was my silliness that saved me.

I knew that sooner or later Jago would make one more attempt to get hold of the will. I was right. If I had thought about things carefully I would have brought Bryn into the house with me, but it's not easy to change your habits. Bryn was a working dog and we never brought him indoors. I put him, as I always did, in his kennel at the end of the cowhouse, and sat down to wait for Jago.

I did not have to wait long. Just before nine I heard him coming down the path. He flung open the door and came in as if he owned the place. He smelt of beer. His eyes went to the shelf where he had left the writing desk and then to me.

"Where've you put that desk?"

"I've put it away."

"You've hidden it, haven't you? And I bet you've got the key as well. Come on, hand it over."

"I won't. You'll never get it. It's not yours. Nothing's yours here."

"We'll see about that!" he shouted.

He reached forward and I felt his hard hands closing around my throat, and touching the chain that hung round my neck. Then he withdrew one hand, pulled out the chain and saw the key fastened at the end of it.

"You sly little ullage — that's where you been keeping it, eh?"

He jerked on the chain, and I felt it biting into my neck, then snapping. The key fell to the ground, and as Jago went down to search for it I saw the dirty white of his scalp showing through the tough red hair. He picked the key up, and, still holding it, struck me on the side of the face. I felt it scrape along my cheek, and the blood begin to run.

"You cunning little bastard! You been keeping this from me, haven' you? Where's that box? Show me where it is or I'll twist your flaming neck off!"

21

His hands closed round my neck again, and I felt that if I didn't find a way of getting rid of him he might kill me.

"It's in the corn bin," I said. "In the stable."

That was all he wanted to know. He dropped his hands and ran out.

There was no sense in waiting for him. He was so far gone with drink and greed that he was capable of anything. I waited till the coast was clear, untied Bryn, and escaped into the darkness. Jago might have the key and the desk but the will was safe in my keeping. There was nothing left for me to do but to run away and hide in some place where Jago couldn't find me, and bide my time.

Chapter 7

On the Run

I slept that night in the open air. It wasn't the first time I had spent a night out of doors. I'd spent many a night on the Fron, not bothering with the cave so that I could be on hand if any of the ewes was in trouble. This time I kept clear of it for another reason. I wanted to be in the open so that if Jago came for me I wouldn't be trapped. I lay down in a sheltered spot I had used many a time before, and with the wall of the rock at my back and Bryn across my legs I kept warm enough, although it turned cold in the night. I lay awake for a long time listening to the owls calling up from the valley, and the sheep coughing. Once I heard something moving over the turf, but it was only a hedgehog. Bryn turned his head to look at it, but left it alone.

As soon as it was light, I got up. There was a queer cold wind blowing across the moor, but I washed my hands and face in the brook, and, more out of habit than anything else, went round the flock to see if everything was all right.

So the morning passed, a cold morning with that strange east wind cutting through everything. Some time before noon I heard the bells of Pentre ringing from the other side of the valley, lower down the river. I knew what they were ringing for. Matty had told me that the vicar's wife was expecting, and the bellringers were going to ring to tell everybody in the parish when the baby came. The thought that everybody in the parish was rejoicing in the birth of a new baby made me feel very lonely. If only some good luck would come my way as well — if only someone would come and tell me that Jago had made up his mind to leave me alone and go away from Talybont. But nobody came.

Then towards midday, after the bells had stopped, I saw

Jago. He was coming up the Fron, not on foot but on a pony. I knew what that meant. He was out to hunt me down.

This was something I had not reckoned on. I knew I could outrun Jago, but I couldn't outrun a mountain pony. I ran for the rocks, talking to Bryn to keep him quiet and close to me. I dodged in and out of the boulders, listening to Jago cursing and whipping the pony backwards and forwards trying to follow me. I knew that, clumsy and stupid though he was, he would run me down in the end, unless I found some way of escape where he could not follow me. At that moment it came to me that there was only one certain way of escape — the waterfall.

I got clear of Jago and made for the Dulas. I scrambled over the first ledge of the fall and stopped for a moment to find if Jago was still following me, and over the noise of the water I could hear the hooves of the pony clattering on the rocks above me. I tried to send Bryn home, but he moved only a few yards away. I could see that he didn't know what to do. I wondered what he would do when I jumped, but I was too concerned about my own safety to spare much thought for him. I jumped down on to the second ledge, and, looking up, saw the figure of Jago outlined against the sky as it had been that night when I had caught him spying on Cefn. I turned away, took a deep breath and leapt, feet foremost, clear of the fall and into the pool. I never felt the impact of the water. All I knew was that I was sinking, that the pool seemed bottomless, and wild currents were pulling at my legs . . . and then I broke surface, and felt myself being carried around in a whirlpool like the lamb I had seen on the first dry day of the Spring. I didn't know whether Jago could see me or not — I could not see him — and to make sure I dived again and swam under water for what I thought was the far end of the pool, found rock under my feet and hauled myself up and out of the water to safety, to see before me the dark and unexplored ravine.

I was shivering now with cold and fright. My clothes were hanging upon me now like lead, but it was out of the question to think of resting. There was no warmth in that cold valley. I knew that I had to find somewhere I could dry my clothes and warm my body, and there was little likelihood of doing either till I got out of the ravine.

It wasn't easy. I had to scramble for more than half a mile over slippery boulders and fallen tree-trunks before I came to a cleft in the gorge with enough footholds for me to climb out of it. I made hard work of getting out. No sunshine reached the bottom of the ravine. My body was chilled and a faint bluish stain was spreading from the ends of my fingers. I began to run, and kept on running, knowing that if I did not get some warmth back into my body anything could happen. The sky had clouded over and there was a cold wind blowing that went straight through my wet clothes.

The moor looked dangerously open, but there was no sign of Jago or Bryn. My legs felt as if they would give way under me, but I knew that if only I could get to the cave I would be safe.

I got there in the end and found the matches where I had left them, and a good supply of dry kindling. The rest of the wood was a bit damp. At first the smoke filled the upper half of the cave so that I couldn't stand upright, but after a while it thinned. I found some stakes and drove them into the floor of the cave, and hung my wet clothes on them. I was so cold that I lay down on the floor to get close to the fire, warming first my back and then my front. I wondered what sort of savage I would look to anyone who might come in and find me there — naked, shivering and grimed with the mud and dust of the cave floor. But my clothes dried out, and the numbness went out of my joints. I was worried about the smoke escaping from the mouth of the cave, and, as soon as I could, I put my trousers on and went out to see if there was anyone searching for me. But my leaping into the pool must have given Jago a shock. There was no sign of him. I had my first meal of the day on the food that I had left in the cave. I didn't stir far from my hide-out for the rest of the day. It was still light when I made up the fire and lay down.

When I woke the next morning it was with the feeling that I knew now what I was going to do, as if something had made up my mind for me while I had been sleeping. There was no question of my giving in to Jago and going back to Talybont. I was on my own; and the strange thing was that I didn't feel lost or abandoned or cheated, but excited.

There was only one thing that worried me. I could not help wondering who would look after my uncle's and aunt's grave. The church at Talybont wasn't used much, but we did not like to neglect our family graves. We had a custom of going out into the fields before Easter Day and bringing back primroses, violets and cowslips and bedding them in the turf over the graves. We called it 'flowering the graves'.

It was looked upon as a shameful thing to neglect the graves at Easter, and it grieved me to think that while all the decent people of Talybont would be paying their respects to their dead relatives there would be no one to put a single flower on our graves.

Chapter 8

A Disappointment

Before Jago had attacked me I had kept hoping that some-how Matty would turn up and come to my help, but I knew that only an unexpected change of plan would bring him on the Fron, because he had told me at the funeral that he had to go to Brecon and would be away for some time. Matty was the only one who had not turned against me, and I felt that if he was not there to help me, I would have to give up Cefn, at least until the time was ripe for me to come back to Talybont and claim it back from Jago. Then at the last minute, almost at the moment when I had made up my mind to go, I remembered Edwin Pugh.

I had met Edwin at the school kept by the old soldier, and had made a friend of him there — or rather he had made a friend of me, for he was older and cleverer than I was. He was the son of a man who made a living by selling muffins in the streets of Builth, but he had no intention of following in his father's footsteps. He always told me that, as soon as he could, he meant to get a position in the new railway that had just been opened from Hereford to Builth, and the last time I had seen him he told me with pride that he had been appointed to take charge of a little station — it was more like a halt than a station — at a place called Bowood. I stood from then on in great awe of him and always thought of him as a young man of great importance, although, as I learnt later, looking after that little halt was a lonely job, and it wasn't everybody that wanted it.

But Edwin, in my eyes, was a person of some influence and since he had never lived in Talybont it struck me that he had perhaps never heard of the charge that had been levelled against me of injuring Evan Lloyd, and would not be prejudiced against me. At school he had always been full of confidence and enterprise, and never at a loss whatever happened. I made up my mind that I would go to Bowood and tell him my story.

Although it was midsummer there was a cold wind blowing on the Fron, and already dry brown leaves were being blown off the mountain ash trees and hollies. The bog cotton flowers were shaking backwards and forwards and as I went past a thorn two crows, that had been feeding on a dead lamb the shepherd had flung into the tree, flew upwards and were whirled away by the wind. But as I dropped down into the valley the wind fell and just before midday I came within sight of Bowood.

I was drawing close to the station when I saw a train sweeping round a curve and Edwin waving his flag to stop it. It drew alongside the platform and Edwin opened a carriage door to let out an elderly well-dressed lady. He lifted his cap to her, and escorted her, with a great show of deference, to the gate, where a groom was waiting for her. Edwin and the lady exchanged a few words. Then she moved on to the victoria, and Edwin ran back to the train. He unloaded some parcels, and loaded fresh ones in their place, then blew his whistle and waved the train off. The engine shot up a plume of brilliant white steam, and the huge oily wheels began to turn. It was the first time I had been close to a train. It was a new thing to me. It was a new thing to all of us in this valley.

For Edwin, though, this was the kingdom he had always meant to possess. He showed me round everything with pride — the waiting room, the ticket office, the station yard, the sidings and the little weighbridge by the side of the yard with its brick cabin and its steelyard. I was wondering when I would get a chance to tell Edwin what I had come to see him for, but he was so excited at having someone to show over his station that I did not dare to interrupt him.

"I've worked hard, Gareth," he said. "But," he added mysteriously, "I've got my reward."

"What kind of reward?"

"Did you see that lady that got out of the train?"

"Yes."

"Do you know who she is?"

"No."

"That's Lady Wallis. She lives at Bowood Court — look, you can see it through the trees. And she's my good angel."

"How?"

"She likes trains. When she goes to Hereford — and London — she uses my station, and I look after her, Gareth. Do you know — she brought her own furniture for this waiting room, and I keep it clean and well-polished for her. Well, she told me one day that her brother was a director of the line, and she was going to speak to him about me. Only today the good news has arrived, and she stopped to congratulate me. Did you see her smiling?"

"What's the good news?"

"Promotion! I leave on Monday."

"Where are you going?"

"I am to be a senior clerk in the station at Hereford!"

"That's good news for you, Edwin."

"Ah, but this is just the beginning. I know how to work hard and how to get on, Gareth. I can make a good job of everything I have to do. I mean to rise — maybe get to Swindon, even Paddington."

"What's Paddington?"

"That's our great London station ... Hullo, what's this?"

We listened and I could make out a faint whistling faraway up the valley.

"It's the goods from Builth. She's due to go through in a few minutes. I tell you, Gareth, it may seem lonely here to a stranger, but there's always something stirring, and when I get to Hereford, then I'll begin to see the world."

We went back to his office and he began to tell me more about his hopes and expectations. I listened to him with a sinking heart. How could I spoil his good news by beginning to speak of my troubles? How could I throw a shadow over his happy day by reciting my misfortunes? How could I expect him to turn away from the contemplation of his own bright future to assist me? In a few days he would be far away. In a few months — who could tell how far he would

29

go? I made up some story about having little to do and wanting to come and see his station, then said goodbye.

At the top of the hill above Bowood I stopped and looked back. Below me I could see a fisherman standing thigh deep in the river, and further upstream a party of ladies and gentlemen were getting out of their boat. They had pulled it up on the shingle. The young women were trying to spread out a tablecloth for their picnic, and I could hear them laughing as the wind caught the edges of the cloth and blew their skirts about their ankles. The young men went backwards and forwards carrying big hampers of food. Then as I stood watching them I heard a train come running along the valley. As it ran clear of the trees I could hear the tickety-tack tickety-tack of its wheels on the track, and the long shrill whistle as it came close to the station. A white column of smoke writhed and twisted above the trees, and as it thinned away in the wind it seemed to be carrying away with it all my hopes of friendship and succour.

On the way home I stopped at a village shop and bought myself some bread and cheese and a knuckle of ham, and though it was heavy to carry, a bottle of stone ginger. There was not much left in the cave, and I knew that until I found somewhere to live I would need all the food I could carry with me.

Chapter 9

The Wild Rover Again

I had no clear idea of where I was going and what I was going to do, but I felt that somewhere in the east I might find freedom and company and work until I felt confident enough to return to Cefn, and challenge Jago. I collected all the food that was left, and the matches, and an old blanket that I used to wrap round me on cold nights, and struck out towards the hills. The moors were covered with rusty bracken and coverts of dark gorse. Sheep were dotted on the slopes like white stones, and little groups of mountain ponies whinnied to their foals as I went past them. Here and there the ground was black with burnt heather sticks, and a few stunted and twisted thorns grew in the gullies.

The weather was dry at first, but as I climbed towards the high mountains the mist came down, and I knew that I had better turn back to lower ground. I remembered the story of the man who had been riding across the forest of Radnor when his horse went over the rocks of Pencwm, and of the boy who had fallen into a mawn-pit and had been sucked under and never seen again. And once a man had tried to walk across the forest without a guide, and when they found him months later there wasn't much left of him, just bones inside his jacket and breeches.

The mist was frightening, but the darkness was almost as bad. As I sat huddled in my old blanket with my back to a stone wall there came into my mind all the stories of ghosts and monsters that we used to tell one another at Talybont — Wild Edric, the headless monster that used to tramp the road between Talybont and Pentre every night, and the witches that used to dance and screech around the old chapel at Maesbleddfa. But somehow I slept and found enough courage to want to go on.

If I had not been so determined, the third day of my flight would have tested me and driven me back to Talybont, Jago or no Jago. A cold night was followed by a showery morning, and it rained on and off most of the day. I made poor progress. I knew that I had to keep dry, and spent precious time sheltering behind walls and stacks waiting for the squalls to pass.

As the light began to go out of the sky I could see that I was in for one more wet night. I could tell by the look of the sky to the north that more bad weather was coming my way. Somewhere or other I would have to find cover, and the sooner I began to look for it the better.

I was lucky. Just before the rain came I saw a small building that looked half like a church and half like a barn standing by itself in a field. The path up to it was overgrown with nettles and brambles, but some one had used it recently. I took it and found, on the blind side of the building, a heavy door with big hinge plates. It was open, and when I went in, I found myself in a church with a raised platform at the far end for a chancel, and high box pews. They were narrow and cramped, but opposite the pulpit was a larger pew, like the squire's pew at Pentre where my aunt once took me to a confirmation service. The wooden floor of the pew was deep in hay and straw. It looked as if the place had been used for a calf pen but there was no muck in it. It was clean and dry, and a heaven-sent lodging.

I still had some food left. It was the custom for the farmers in our part of the world to give refreshment to any poor people who asked for it, especially at Michaelmas. A farmer's wife about ten miles north of Talybont had given me some cheese and cold bacon and had let me pick up a few windfall apples, and I had pulled a few small turnips from a field farther on. I ate a little and then settled down in the straw and hay.

I can remember dreaming in a vague way of something connected with a story my aunt had once told me about a boy who had lost his way in a wood and woke to find a bear sleeping beside him. I opened my eyes. I could see nothing, but I thought I could hear a pew door being opened and someone or something settling down on the floor. I lay awake for a few moments wondering if I should get up and try to find what it was that had disturbed me, but I was very sleepy. I shut my eyes and did not open them again till the light coming in through the big chancel window waked me, and I saw peering down at me from the side of the pew a vast tousled head, like the head of a giant. I jumped up in alarm, but the stranger put out a huge arm to restrain me, and smiled at me.

"So — you're the young shaver that's been sleeping in my bed, eh?"

"I didn't know it was yours. I didn't know it was any-body's."

"Well, maybe, to tell the truth, it *is* anybody's. But it's my straw. You're lucky I was in a loving mood and didn't kick you out. You gave me a surprise, boy. Did you hear me come in?"

"Yes."

"But you didn't let on, did you? You kept mum. Very cunning! Very sly!"

"I was tired."

"What are you doing sleeping in places like this? You on the pad?"

"What?"

"Tramping. On the road."

"No."

"I thought not. You don't look to me like a young feller that's used to mouching. What's happened?"

"I've run away."

"Somebody chucked you out, eh?"

"Yes."

"You tell me your story, boy. You tell me while we're having our breakfast — if we have any to get. What have you got in them pockets?"

"Cheese and cold bacon and a bit of bread."

"Very good. Very sumptuous. Let's have it in style."

"Where?"

"Here. There's a table, isn't there? I don't have my grub

on a table every day of the week."

"But it's a communion table, isn't it?"

"Then we'll take communion together. I don't suppose the old man will object."

"Which old man?"

"Him above. He won't mind. It's his house, isn' it? Come on. Dish the grub up and tell me your story."

I didn't tell him everything. I told him about my aunt and her wish, and about Jago and the way he had driven me out of the house, but I didn't tell him that I had my aunt's will sewn away in my belt. And there was something else I didn't tell him — that I had seen him before. He was the stranger that I had heard singing the song about the Wild Rover in the Swan.

"It's a rum yarn," he said when I had finished, "but it's not the first I've listened to. What's your name?"

"Gareth."

"And a very nice name. You call me Tom. Tom Hard-up — that's what they call me on the road. I may be short of cash now and then but I'm never short of hard-up. I'll just have a puff and then we'll see what the weather's like."

He struck a match on the table top and lit his pipe.

"What's your plan now, Gareth?"

"I'm going to find work."

"I won't be much help to you in that line."

"Don't you work then?"

"What — me work? Never."

"How do you live then?"

"You must be green, boy, if you think a chap's got to work to keep alive. I've never worked in my life, and I'm not going to start now. I been a rover ever since I can remember. I don't mind where I eat and where I sleep as long as I'm a free man and somebody else does the slaving. I know where to find friends. And I'm going to take you to see one of them this very day — if that flaming rain has stopped."

"Am I coming with you?"

"Of course you are. You got the sawney, haven' you?"

"The what?"

"Never mind, you'll learn."

Talybont was a small place, but I had never been lonely there. There had always been someone to greet and someone to talk to. In the evening my aunt always wanted to know what had happened during the day, and after she had gone to bed there was the Swan and all the men coming and going. Even on the Fron I had never felt lonely. Ever since that day when Jago had driven me away I had felt abandoned. I had spoken to no one, and no one had spoken to me since I had passed that hill farm where the farmer's wife helped me. For the first time in my life I knew what it was like to be an outcast. But when Tom offered to take me with him I felt that I had found a friend again, a man who was prepared to be kind to me, perhaps to stand by me. After days of loneliness, idleness and misery he seemed to come into my life like a deliverer.

Chapter 10

On the Road

Tom set off at a great pace, and it was all I could do to keep up with him. Most of the way was by sheep track to begin with, and we had to go single file, but even when the path broadened, I had the feeling that he didn't want to talk any more. Whenever I tried to catch up with him, he quickened his pace and put me behind him again. He said nothing about the way we were taking, and what we were making for. My main memory of that long walk was of his enormous legs striding before me, and his heavy boots coming down heartily, mile after mile on stones, on clumps of heather, on wet spongy turf. I felt that I was almost fettered to those legs, and to follow them mile after mile was like working at a treadmill.

But about midday he stopped, shaded his eyes and began to scan the landscape. We had come to a green lane, with the remains of stone walling on either side and thorns growing between the stones, and the lane led towards a little farm with a green door, peat stacks in a yard, and white patches of washing drying on the bushes. Half a mile away from the house a man in a grey shirt was working on the hillside, cutting fern.

"Time for a rest," said Tom, speaking for the first time since we had set off. "There's the man of the house off the premises. Let's go and see if his wife has any good in her heart. You afraid of dogs?"

"No."

"Right. You go first then. I don't like dogs and they don' like me overmuch."

I could not understand why he was so timid. The only dog that came out to meet me was an old brown spaniel that barked once or twice, then backed away. Seeing that there was no danger, Tom pushed ahead of me, but a turkey cock that was pecking outside the door suddenly flew up at him, and he backed away in alarm.

"Damn that thing," he shouted. "Get rid of it afore it has my eyes out! I mortally hate things that fly up at me like that." And it was only when he was sure that it was out of range that he brought himself to knock on the door.

It was opened by a young woman with flour on her hands. She was slightly built, like a true Welsh girl, and she had to crane her neck to look up at Tom.

"Good morning to you, ma'm," said Tom. "It's a fine day for your washing day, isn't it?"

"Isn't it lovely now?" she replied. "And after all that terrible rain we had yesterday. I'm doing my washing and my baking on the same day for once. Has that turkey cock been having a go at you?"

"He just made a little jump at us."

"Isn't he a terrible turkey cock now? When we first came here I couldn't stop him flying at me and trying to stock me. You wouldn't believe it but when I first went out to feed the fowls I had to put a scuttle over my head. Go on, get away with you! I think he's the best watch dog we've got."

She smiled as she spoke, as if she was glad to have some one to talk to. Living in this lonely farm she must have had few callers.

"I was wondering," said Tom, "if you would be so kind as to give the boy and me a drop of something to drink just to wet our mouths. We're as dry as a bone walking over these hills."

"Indeed I can. It's parching work walking these hills on a warm day. Have you come far then?"

"A tidy step. I've been working on the hay harvest down beside Brecon, but you know what it is. Once the job's finished you soon get turned off. But I got a letter to a man down beside Hereford and we'll get taken on there."

"Just you sit down and rest your legs for a few minutes. I'll bring you a mug of cider — or maybe your son would like a drop of milk."

37

"Milk would be fine for him, but the cider would be very welcome for me."

She went indoors, and as soon as she had turned her back Tom got up.

"Just you keep your eye on that turkey," he said, and he slipped into the barn that stood at right angles to the farmhouse. Whatever he was looking for he must have found quickly, for he was back before the woman returned.

"I got out that letter from the man in Brecon," he said. "I thought you might like to have a look at it. Just to show that we are bona fides."

"Oh it's no good showing me that," said the woman, laughing. "I couldn't read a word of it, even if it was in Welsh. Sit down now and help yourself to a bit of this pie."

"A thousand thanks to you. I can go hungry and never feel it, but I don' like to see a boy go too long on an empty belly."

"Poor lad, he looks as if he could do with something inside him. My husband gets like this at lambing time. He's up all hours of the day and night and he gets as thin as a rake. I have to feed him up again as soon as it's over. I'm always telling him that this farm is a bit too big for one man. He could do with a bit of help but where are you to get it from in an out-of-the-way place like this? I'll put something up for you both to keep you going till you get down to Hereford."

"Tom," I said, when we had said goodbye to the kind shepherd's wife, "why did you tell her I was your son?"

"You've got the wrong end of the stick, boy. I never said you were my son. It was she that said it, not me."

"But you didn't contradict her, did you?"

"Don't you ask too many questions about what I do. Just you keep mum and leave the talking to me."

"What did you go into the barn for?"

"Gareth, you strike me sometimes like a young feller with a good headpiece, but you don't take too much notice at times, do you? When I said no questions, I meant it. So just you shut up when I tell you and keep your trap shut till I tell you to open it."

It wasn't long before I learnt what he had been up to in

38

the barn. A few miles further on he stopped at a place where we had to cross a brook. It was a place that he seemed to have stayed in before. He lit a fire, pulled out a rusty tin from under a bush, filled it and dropped half a dozen eggs into it.

"I told you you'd find out what I'd been doing if only you waited long enough. Wait till that water boils and then count two hundred slowly. Then take them out, and if you're sensible I'll give you one or two."

Chapter 11

The Mad Priest

At last we stopped on the top of a rise, and Tom pointed downwards.

"There you are. That's our kip of the next few days. And that's where our friend hangs out."

"It's a church."

"Of course it is. Not the first one you've slept in, is it? Only tonight you'll have a bit more company than usual."

It was an old church, neglected and almost in ruins. The grey stone walls were all stippled with patches of yellow lichen, like rosettes, and the slates had begun to fall from the roof. The lower parts of the walls were blackened in places, as if somebody had been lighting fires up against them, and just outside the porch there was a big yew tree that was splitting open with age and neglect. It had a big hollow in it like the place where a statue of a saint could be put. The overgrown churchyard was almost filled with men and women, sitting on the tombstones or with their backs against the walls. It looked as if resurrection day had come and people had come out of their graves and were waiting to be summoned to something.

We went down the slope, and as soon as Tom went through the gate into the churchyard the men got up and touched their caps, and the women gave him a little curtsey, but in an offhand way as if they had no great heart in what they were doing. There was only one man who failed to salute him, a wild looking man in a ragged overcoat who was parading up and down the church path, flinging his arms about and making unintelligible noises. Tom waited for him to salute him but the man went on gesturing and muttering.

"Where's your manners?" shouted Tom, seizing him by the neckerchief and pulling him forward. "Have you forgotten the rules here?"

The man suddenly stopped muttering, and looked up at Tom like a schoolboy caught in some misdeed and expecting to be cuffed for it. Then he pulled off his cap.

"That's better! That's manners now, that is," said Tom. "Just you remember what you have to do when you see me, or else you'll get a taste of this!"

He pushed his great nobbly fist up against the man's nose, then suddenly opened his hand, pushed him, sent him sprawling and walked over him.

"There's your company, Gareth," he said. "Macers and mouchers and mumpers, every one of them."

I had seen plenty of beggars before — my aunt had a constant stream of them calling on her, and two or three passed through Talybont every week — but never so many in one company. There were five or six women sitting together in a sheltered corner made by the walls of the main church and the porch, swarthy, weather-beaten women with creased and wrinkled faces and shiny black hair. One of them was rubbing some kind of oil into her scalp and twisting her hair into tight ringlets. Another was looking through her neighbour's head, cracking with her horny fingernail the lice she combed out. A third was smoking a short clay pipe and passing it every now and then to a younger woman who seemed to be her daughter.

The men sat apart from the women, silent and listless. One was stretched out on a tombstone as motionless as an effigy. Two others, who looked so alike that I thought they must be twin brothers, were going through a dirty wallet they had put down beside them, and were nibbling at dirty carrots and turnips they kept pulling out of the bag. An old man near them kept opening and shutting his mouth and working the muscles of his face as if he was going to say something, but nothing came. The man that Tom had knocked down had gone back to his lunatic gesturing and groaning. While I watched him he went over to the yew tree, and stood inside the hollow, in the attitude of a bishop or a saint blessing his flock.

By this time Tom had gone his rounds. He came back to the man who was playing the fool in the tree.

41

"You're a flaming lunatic, aren' you?" he said. "Come on, stop that blasted play-acting and go and tell Mr Price that I've come and he can start any time now. Come on, get on with it!"

The man disappeared through the churchyard gate. Then I heard the bell ringing and Tom called me over to follow him. One of the women held the door open for us and we went into the church.

Talybont church was a neglected place, but it was a temple compared with this dirty old barn-like place. There were holes in the ceiling, and big dirty stains on the walls where the rain came in. There were panes missing from the windows and the holes were stuffed with dirty rags and straw. The whole place smelt of candle grease and candle smoke, paraffin, dirt and stale food. The floor was littered with crusts and bones, and somebody had been sick just in front of the broken altar rails and nobody had cleaned it up. There was another big oily stain in the middle of the aisle that smelt as if somebody had spilt a can of paraffin. Most of the pew doors were missing and there were torn prayer books everywhere, their loose pages sticking like damp leaves to the wet flagstones.

It looked as if we were assembling for some kind of service — exactly what kind of service I had no idea. To tell the truth I did not know much about church services at all, except Holy Communion which my aunt had used to take me to at Easter and Christmas. I made up my mind to keep my eye on Tom and do what he did. I was so much at sea here that I looked to him for everything.

Suddenly I saw him getting to his feet. The parson had come in through the vestry door.

I had never seen any priest like him. He was more like an apparition than a priest — like someone out of a book of ghost stories — a gaunt man with a long lean dirty face, dressed in a soiled surplice with a great tear under the right armpit, and boots caked with mud. His long hands were as dirty as his face, with long black streaks down the backs of them. He had a strange vacant look on his face as if he was sleepwalking, as if he was in some kind of trance and hardly knew what he was doing. He walked over to his lectern. There was a bible in front of him, but he did not bother to open it. Instead in a spectral yet musical voice he began upon a passage that I was never to forget. It was his anthem, hardly a day was to pass without my hearing him recite it.

"A certain man made a great supper, and bade many. And he sent his servant at supper time to say to them that were bidden, 'Come, for all things are now ready'. And they all with one consent began to make excuse. The first said, 'I have bought a piece of ground and I must needs go and see it: I pray thee, have me excused'. And another said, 'I have bought five yoke of oxen, and I go to prove them: I pray thee, have me excused'. And another said, 'I have married a wife and therefore I cannot come'.

So the servant came and shewed his Lord all these things. Then the master of the house, being angry, said to his servant, 'Go quickly into the streets and lanes of the city, and bring in hither the poor, the maimed and the halt and the blind'.

And the servant said, 'Lord it is done as thou hast commanded, and still there is room'.

And the Lord said unto the servant, 'Go out into the highways and hedges and compel them to come in, that my house may be filled.

For I say unto you, that none of those men who were bidden shall taste of my supper'."

Then when he came to the end of his recitation, he gave out the number and the first line of a hymn, one that I had often heard the Methodists of Talybont singing. It was 'Onward Christian Soldiers'. Some of the tramps made a show of reading from their books, but I don't think they could really follow the words on the page. Nor did they really know the tune and there was no organist to give us a note or keep us together. Someone — maybe it was Tom — started us off, and I could hear his strong voice above the dreadful howling and bellowing that came from the rest of the congregation, but neither Tom nor the parson seemed to be put out. They waited till the din had subsided and then went on to the next part of the service.

It was a kind of communion service: that is, it began like a service for the administering of the Holy Sacrament, but ended as I had never known any other service to end. When the priest held up the holy wafers, the tramps went swarming up to the broken communion rails, jostling and pushing for a place. They held out their hands for the wafers but threw them away or spat them out as soon as they had received them, but they took long swallows of the holy wine, spilling it greedily over their cheeks and chins. Then, when the wafers had been given out and the wine drunk, the priest went from one person to another giving out sixpences. It was Tom who took charge at this point, making sure that everyone was paid and no one cheated, pushing the men and women away from the communion rails as soon as they had had their due. Then, when all had been paid, the priest said, "Let not those who live in sin neglect this opportunity to make their union honourable and lovely in the sight of the Lord. Before I pronounce the benediction and our feast begins, are there any men and women in this congregation here present who desire to be joined in holy matrimony?"

"Yes, Mr Price," said Tom, stepping forward. "We've got two customers here for you today. Come on, Bella, and you, Nosey. Get yourselves ready for the ceremony, and ... "

"Bella's been married before," shouted someone.

"So's Nosey!"

"Shut your traps, all of you," shouted Tom. "This is a serious service and you'd better treat it as serious or else you'll pay for it. Come on, let's have the ring, whoever has it."

"Here it is, Tom," said one of the women I had seen sitting by the porch. As soon as it was produced, all the congregation began singing the wedding march, or rather bawling out some wordless tune that sounded more or less like it, and the bride and bridegroom set off arm in arm up to the communion rails.

Chapter 12

After the Wedding

When the service was over Mr Price turned and sank down with his head resting on the altar as if he had collapsed. I could not make out if he was praying or had fallen into some kind of faint, but the newly married couple took no notice of him. Nor did any of the others in the congregation. The bride and bridegroom came strutting down the aisle, like children in a play, and as they came the tramps all began to sing

> Now you're married I wish you joy,
> First a girl and then a boy . . .

and then somebody started on another song

> I am a young maid truly,
> And I live down the street,
> And I thought to marry a fair young man
> To warm my back and feet.

> But I have married a roving man.
> He never says his prayers.
> He's an ugly body, a bubbly body,
> He kicks me down the stairs.

I had never heard people sing and play the fool in church like this before, and I expected Mr Price to get up and tell the tramps to remember where they were, but he remained slumped at the altar. It was Tom who silenced them.

"That'll do for the moment! Let's have a bit of order, now. Well, friends and fellow mouchers, as you've all seen our kind patron Mr Price has turned up trumps again. So let's have all your money in the kitty. Come on, Bella and

Nosey, wedding money as well. Hand it over to Willie. It's Willie's turn to get the grub and the lush. There you are, Willie — the money's all yours, and you should know what to do with it. The pothouse is open, and they're waiting for you. But it's Willie's first time, folks. So we'd better tell what happens to anybody who tries monkey tricks, shall we? Shall we tell him the story of Ananias and Sapphira? Shall we ask Mr Price to tell it?"

All this time Mr Price remained on his knees, with his head on the altar table, as still as if it had been glued to the stone.

"You tell it, Tom! You tell it!" shouted the tramps.

"All right. Here we go then. The story of Ananias and Sapphira! This is specially for you, Willie, and for any mean skunk who tries to be gammy in this company."

He went over to the lectern and pretended to throw open the pages of the bible, but I could see that he was not reading from it.

"A certain man, named Ananias, with Sapphira, his wife, sold a possession . . . and then what did he do?"

"HE KEPT BACK PART OF THE PRICE!" shouted the tramps. I could tell that this was a kind of game with them. They knew what Tom was going to say and how to answer him.

"Right," he went on, "he kept back part of the price. But Peter said, Ananias, why hath Satan filled thine heart to lie to the Holy Ghost and keep back part of the price? And Ananias, hearing these words, fell down. And what did he do?"

"HE GAVE UP THE GHOST!"

"Right," said Tom, "he gave up the ghost, and the young men rose and wound him up and carried him out and buried him. And what did his wife, Sapphira do as well?"

"SHE KEPT BACK PART OF THE PRICE!"

"And what happened to her?"

"SHE GAVE UP THE GHOST!"

"Yes, she gave up the ghost, and the young men came in and found her dead, and carrying her forth, buried her by her husband. So now you know, Willie, what happens to anybody who tries to be cokum and play tricks, don't you? Off you go. And now, my fellow mouchers, until Willie comes back we'll carry on with our own service. Where's the robe, Sal?"

One of the women who clearly knew what was expected of her, went over to one of the pews and pulled out from under the seat a big tattered robe, as big as the robe I had once seen the parson at Pentre wearing at Easter, but full of holes and caked with dirt like the hem of Mr Price's cassock. She went behind Tom and another woman came up to help her, and they pulled out the folds of the robe like somebody pulling out the wings of a bird he is thinking of buying. Then they tied it round his neck, and Sal, taking a little tin from the pocket of her skirt, proceeded to put some colour, like the reddle we used on the ewes, on his lips and cheeks. When she had finished, I didn't know whether he looked like a clown or a woman or a king in a pageant. But no one laughed. The robing was done very seriously, though Mr Price saw nothing of it and still knelt at the altar as if he had been struck down there and couldn't lift his head. When the women had finished with him Tom lifted his arms up and cried out

"Long live the Worshipful Company of the Ragged Rovers!" They set up a great cheer and all broke out into singing. Above their funny howling singing I could hear Tom's voice, the pure strong voice I had first heard at the Swan

We are the jolly rovers,
We ramble up and down.
We don't care a cus wherever we be
In country or in town.

We cannot work, we cannot pray,
We've all got mange and itch.
We booze and we guzzle and we scratch and we stink
And we sleep like frogs in a ditch.

But we don't care whatever we do,
We're jolly roving men.

47

> We'll do it here and we'll do it there,
> And we'll do it again and again.

The rigmarole, Tom's bible story and their shouts as they followed it, the putting on of the robe and the singing — all these seemed to breathe new life into the beggars. They lost that depressed and beaten look they had all worn when I had first seen them. They bawled and yelled, and began to get excited and gay. Then when Willie arrived with the food and the drink, the women got out the stoves and lit them. Pans and kettles appeared and the smell of eggs and bacon began to fill the church. I looked up to see what Mr Price was doing and saw that he had come to, and was standing at the communion rails with a foolish smile on his face. He tried to say grace but nobody took any notice of him. As for me I thought I had never in my life smelt anything so delicious as the smell of the eggs and bacon frying. I sat down with Sal and her friend and ate as I had not eaten for a long time. All round me the gaiety had turned to greedy guzzling and shouting and bawling, but I hardly noticed it. I had not felt so free and happy since the days before Jago had come to torment me. I ate and drank and joined in the dancing and the tomfoolery that followed until I could keep awake no more. I rolled under a pew, not caring whether I had anything to wrap round me or not, and sank into sleep.

When I woke the next morning, I saw all the tramps and beggars lying around me like soldiers who had fallen in some battle. Mr Price was not with them, but Tom was sprawled out with his back against the pulpit and his arm round Sal, his face still smudged with the dabs of red colour with which the women had painted him.

During the next few weeks whenever a service was held it was followed by a feast. The sixpences were paid out, the food was bought and cooked, Tom was robed and crowned King of the Beggars and the drinking and singing went on till everyone fell asleep. After a while I grew less and less reluctant to join in, and would have been disappointed if the ceremony had not taken place. Mr Price never seemed to care what was happening so long as his guests were happy, and I took my cue from him. More than that, I began to look forward to each jollification. Service days were red letter days and I looked forward to them as I had to market days at Builth and noisy evenings in the Swan after the sheep sales.

Chapter 13

I Find a Home

I had slept soundly, but this time when I woke the smell of beer and stale tobacco smoke made me feel sick. I stepped over the sleepers and went out into the churchyard and up the hill. It was a fine dry morning. Just above the horizon lay a long low cloud, and between the edge of the cloud and the rim of the mountains shone a pale golden light. The air was pure and fresh.

When I came down from the hill, I found that the women were up and making cans of tea on their stoves. Tom was sitting in the warm corner by the church porch eating slices of bread and butter and drinking from a pint pot.

"Well, my boy," he said to me pleasantly, "how did you enjoy the bust-up, eh?"

"Very much. I'm a bit swimmy this morning, that's all."

"You haven't been brought up properly, boy, that's your handicap. I bet that aunt of yours was a bit strait-laced, what?"

"She was very good-living."

"I bet she never came across a parson like ours, did she?"

"Is he a real parson?"

"Of course he is. Why shouldn't he be?"

"He doesn't look like one, and he doesn't behave like one, does he?"

"Don' you worry about that, boy. He's a saint, is Mr Price, and he's goin' to look after you, Gareth. Yes. You. I told you he'd be your friend, didn' I? I've fixed it up with him. I have to keep going off here and there and doing things, see, but you'll be all right with him. He's not poor, you know."

"I thought he was."

"Oh no. He's got money of his own. That's how he pays

us to come to his services. If you play your cards properly, boy, you'll be in clover there."

As soon as he had had his smoke he took me over to the vicarage. It was a tiny house of dark stone patched here and there with dull bricks, and the red patches and peeling white-wash gave it the look of a mangy dog. The chimney stack had a big crack running almost from top to bottom, and tufts of grass were growing out of the guttering. The windows were all out and rough planks had been nailed across the frames and the door was nearly off its hinges. Three cherry trees covered with green fruit were standing knee-deep in the brambles and nettles that filled the garden.

Mr Price was sitting just inside the door looking at some papers he had spread out on a box that he was using for a desk. He looked up as if his mind was far away and he hardly recognised Tom.

"I brought you the boy I was telling you about, Mr Price. Here he is. Gareth's the name."

"You are very welcome, Gareth."

"Gareth here will be no trouble to you, Mr Price. He's been well brought-up. He'll be company for you. He'll be a disciple to you, Mr Price. Shall I show him where he kips?"

"Yes do that, Tom. Very kind of you."

So it was that I moved into the vicarage. It was the dirtiest house I had ever seen. The walls had once been white-washed, but now they were blackened with soot and spotted with fly-dirt. There were only two rooms, but hardly any light came into either because the windows were boarded up. One was furnished with an old table and a tea-chest that Mr Price used as a desk, and the other was bedroom and kitchen in one, and more of the former than the latter because Mr Price never seemed to do any cooking. He ate no proper meals except those the tramp-women made and those he took at nearby farmhouses. His bed was a dirty mattress, and mine a heap of straw full of ticks that bit me and kept me awake. After the first night I threw the straw out and made myself a new bed in Mr Price's study.

Mr Price did not seem to notice what I was doing to tidy the place up a little. One day he told me that before he came to the vicarage he had lived in three bathing machines he had bought from a man in Aberystwyth, and he promised to show me where he had kept them, but he forgot. He had a bad memory for most things and at times hardly knew what he was doing or saying. He never washed and never took off his clothes. He used to go to bed even without taking off his boots or his old mittens.

On my second night in his house I went to bed leaving him sitting before the fire reading and making notes. I must not have got rid of all the fleas because I kept waking and seeing Mr Price's rushlight still burning. Then I heard a voice, and I thought at first it was the voice of someone who had chosen to call on the parson in the middle of the night but, twisting round on my palliasse to look through the doorway, I saw the figure of Mr Price himself, sitting up in bed, his mittened hands folded together as if in prayer. I thought he must have wakened, as I had read of monks doing, to perform some office or other, but I could not properly make out what he was saying and caught only snatches of it.

"I, Lord, John Price, Master of Arts of the University of Cambridge ... this forsaken place ... I have taken upon myself the garb of humility ... forgive ... thy mean and unworthy servant ... the light of thy countenance, Lord ... Amen."

Then he sank back in his bed and slept, and I got up and put out his rushlight for him.

The next night I heard him again. He sounded to me like a man who was trying to defend himself. Maybe he was trying to explain to God why it was that he allowed such strange things to happen in his church. I thought I heard him going over it all the next night, but I could not be sure. Perhaps he went over it every night. I never knew. I ceased to be disturbed by it. I never mentioned his strange habit to him and he never spoke of it to me. I suspected that he knew as little about what happened during the night as he did about what happened during the day.

Chapter 14

Broken Promises

Most of the people in Mr Price's parish were Methodists, and held their services in a chapel they had built a mile or so away on a cold hillside. Mr Price had therefore no parish visits to make, and he spent most of his time walking by himself, reading and making notes. Since no light came through the boarded windows of his house, he had the habit of dragging out the box that was his desk into the doorway, so that I had to push past him every time I went in and out, but he never complained of being disturbed. He never complained of anything. He was the most forgiving and forbearing man I had ever met.

Where he slept, what he drank and what he ate — these things were of no importance to him. He was grateful to me for washing his bedclothes, but it would never have occurred to him to wash them himself. He ate whatever food was given to him by the tramp women or by farm-wives, or whatever I prepared for him. When I asked him for money to buy provisions he would fish in his pocket and put all the coins he found there in my hand. Tom told me that in addition to his stipend Mr Price had a private income, but how his money came to him and where he kept it was a mystery.

He was a silent absent-minded companion, given to talking only half-audibly to himself, and to covering sheet after sheet with mysterious signs. It was some time before I learnt what they were.

"Gareth," he said, "did you go to school? Can you read?"

"Yes, sir."

"And can you write?"

"Yes, sir, reasonably well."

"But writing is a slow business, isn't it? That is, writing as most people write. It takes too long. But I've invented a new style of writing. Have you ever heard of shorthand?"

"No, sir."

"I'll tell you. There are many styles of shorthand, you know, but I've dismissed them, all of them. I have invented a new system. It's easy to learn and it's easy to read. What do you think of this?"

He showed me a sheet of paper covered with illegible signs.

"I can't understand it."

"In this tiny compass — look, just the first few lines — what do you think is contained?"

"I don't know."

"The first chapter of the Book of Genesis! Look at the chapter in the Bible — here it is — and then look at my version. One tenth of the space. Isn't that wonderful?"

"But how do you read it, Mr Price?"

"A little patience, a little study, and then think of the advantages, Gareth. A man can carry the Bible around in his waistcoat pocket. He can fold up a gospel in the back of his watch."

"How long does it take to learn to read it?"

"That's what I am going to find out. Because I want you to be my pupil, Gareth. You'll be my pupil and you'll be my disciple. My first ... my first ... "

I waited for him to finish his sentence, but something else seemed to have come into his mind. He went inside for a book, opened it and began to scribble on a new sheet of paper.

"Mr Price," I said, "when do you want me to ... ?"

But I got no answer from him. Nor did he ever return to his plan to teach me his shorthand. Whatever design he had of making me his first disciple went out of his mind as soon as it had come into it. He relapsed into silence.

This was not the only proposal that came to nothing: another came from Tom. Most of the tramps were a bit wary of me at first and behaved as if they didn't know quite what to make of me and how far to trust me, but Tom took me under his wing. He looked after me and amused me and made me forget that I was alone.

"It's a good job you've fallen in with me, Gareth. I'll give you a good training, and you'll be able to look after yourself. You'll be a real nobbler afore you're finished."

"What's that?"

"A real sharp."

"I still don't follow you."

"I'll teach you. You'll have to get the lingo off, won' you, or else these fellers will smell you a mile off, and they'll strip you naked afore you know where you are. It's their mother tongue, boy, and if you're going on the pad it had better be yours as well."

"I don't think I'll go on the pad."

"Don't be stupid. You don't know what's good for you, that's your trouble. I been on it all my life and it's done me no harm, has it? You'll make a better living on the pad than you would looking after sheep all day."

In spite however of his promise to give me lessons something seemed to happen to make him lose interest in them. Worse than that he was at times irritable and quarrelsome, and one day when he could see that I'd failed to understand some word he'd used he flared up at me.

"For God's sake, use your grey matter!" he shouted. "Be a bit sharper on the uptake, will you? I'm beginning to think you're a bit on the stupid side." At times like these he reminded me of Jago, but it wasn't often he lost his temper. He was the first man, since my uncle died, who took an interest in me.

It was easy to see how Tom had come to be the King of the Beggars. Most of the tramps were thin and underfed, and they complained constantly of sore throats and bad coughs, and aches and pains in their legs. Compared with them, Tom was a giant of a man, very strong in the arms, heavily built and fresh coloured. The beggars could be sharp and cunning when they were lying and cheating, but more often than not they were slow-witted and dull; but Tom was never at a loss no matter what he was up to. Where they were, more often than not, confused and stupid, he was clear minded. When they got drunk and tried to sing, they bawled and yelled and muddled words and tune, but Tom was a fine singer and never forgot either.

On wet nights when they collected for shelter in the church, after they had had something to drink, they would get him to sing, and as soon as I heard him I would go back into the church just to listen to him. He knew a vast number of songs — 'The Cock Fight', 'The Deserter from Kent', 'The Moucher and the Milkmaid', 'The Man from Burningham Town', and, best of all, 'The Wild Rover'. This was the song he always finished with. I noticed that after he had sung that he would sing no more that night.

One night I heard him singing and went in to listen to him. There wasn't much to drink because Mr Price had run out of funds and he hadn't had a service for days. For once the tramps seemed sober and serious. All they wanted was to listen to Tom. So he sang on and on — 'The Deserter from Kent', 'Jack the Jolly Tar', 'Come all ye Tramps and Begging Lads', 'The Manchester Angel', 'The Liverpool Packet'. Something must have come over him that night. Something must have come over us all. I knew nothing about singing. The only singing I knew was what I had heard in church or at the Swan, and I daresay a good musician could have found many a fault with Tom's voice. But to me he was the finest singer I had ever heard. His voice filled the whole dusty church, and when he came to his favourite — 'The Wild Rover' — you could have heard a pin drop. The beggars were not good listeners as a rule — they couldn't stop fidgeting and arguing — but for once a mood of seriousness and penitence came over us all, and I saw some of the women crying. Even Mr Price left his books and came in to listen, and I saw him standing at the back of the church with that foolish look that so often came over him.

When the singing was over and the women had lit their stoves, Tom came over to me and sat down.

"You like that song, don't you, Tom?"

"Yes, that's my song, Gareth. My special. Nobody sings that one but me."

"Do you really mean it?"

"Mean what?"

"What the song says. That you'll give up being a rover."

"Why shouldn' I?"

"I thought you liked being on the pad."

"I do. But you have to think of the future, haven't you? I'm not as young as I was, Gareth. And when I look at some of these old coves here it makes me think."

"Think what?"

"Maybe it was time I was thinking of settling down. Do you know what I sometimes think I would like?"

"What?"

"A place of my own, Gareth. A place I could settle down in, like you will."

"Like Cefn?"

"Yes."

"If ever I get it."

"Of course you will. One of these fine days, you'll go back there. And maybe I'll be there with you."

"Living with me?"

"Why not? We could be nice and cosy there, couldn' we? I could look after you, Gareth. How would you like that?"

"It would be nice."

"You could make a living there. And I could look after you, couldn' I? You wouldn' have any Jagos coming to put you out if I was there, would you? I would look after your interests. You've never had anybody to stick up for you, have you?"

"No."

"But I would. We could be very snug, you and me, boy. We could be good partners. So all we have to do, see, is to find some way of getting that place. Jago's got no right to it. It was left to you. You told me that, didn't you?"

"My aunt said it was mine."

"That's the ticket. All we have to do now, is to see that you get your rights, and that's what I'm going to do, boy."

I was on the brink of telling him that I knew how I could get my rights — I had the will, and all that I wanted was someone to stand by me and face Jago and all the rest of the people of Talybont — but I didn't. I don't know why I did

57

not tell him there and then that I had the proof of my inheritance in my belt and could show it to him, but something warned me to be cautious and to wait. What it was I could not tell, but it was strong enough to make me hold back and hold my tongue.

Chapter 15

Secrets

I did not always control my tongue so well. A few days later I forgot myself and unwisely revealed something that I ought to have kept to myself.

"Here, Gareth," said Tom, "sit down here for a bit. I want to ask you something. What was the name of that place you said you lived in?"

"Cefn."

"No, not the name of the house. The village."

"That was Talybont."

"There's a pub there, isn't there? The Swan."

"Yes, Mrs Priddy's."

"I been in that place."

"I know you have."

"How do you know that?"

"I saw you there one night. After the sale at Pentre. I heard you singing there one night."

"What were you doing there?"

"I wasn't inside. Mrs Priddy wouldn't let us in. I was outside. I saw you go in. And I saw you come out. You stopped to look at a man lying drunk in the road."

"Not me, boy."

"You did, I saw you."

"It must have been somebody else."

"I'm sure it was you."

"You got a good memory, Gareth, and you're a sharp little cove. You know a lot of things, don't you, that you keep to yourself, but you got the wrong end of the stick this time. You got hold of the wrong individual, boy. You want to watch yourself. You'll be getting so sharp you'll cut yourself one of these days."

He changed the conversation. I was certain that he was the man I had seen coming out of Mrs Priddy's house, but he was just as certain that I was mistaken. Maybe something had happened that night that he didn't want anybody to know about. In any case it wasn't my business, and I could sympathise with him for not wanting strangers to pry into his secrets. After all I had my own.

Nevertheless I found it more difficult to keep them to myself. Tom was a very persistent questioner. Later in the day he took me into the church, shut the door and began to question me.

"What was this aunt of yours like that you used to live with? Susannah Phillips — is that what they called her? Was she well-off?"

"I don't know. We never talked about money."

"But you always had plenty, didn't you? For food. For clothes. You got a good pair of boots there, and that jacket of yours cost a penny. What did you pay for them?"

"My aunt always paid. We didn't buy much."

"How about the money from the lambs? The ones you sold at Builth, was it?"

"I never handled that. I suppose the farmers and butchers who bought them sent her the money."

"Did she put it in the Penny Bank — or somewhere like that?"

"I don't know. I don't think so. She never went to the Penny Bank because that was in Pentre."

"She must have kept it in the house then. Did she keep it in a tin or something like that?"

"I think she kept some in her writing desk."

"But Jago's got the key for that, hasn't he? Didn't you tell me he got it off you? Why didn't you take the money afore he got his hands on it?"

"It wasn't mine."

"Of course it was yours! She left you everything, didn't she? You've been a bit of a chump, haven't you? Your aunt had a farm and a flock of sheep and a tidy bit of money tucked away as well — and you just chucked it away! You let a fortune slip through your fingers — enough to keep us in clover for the rest of our days."

He disturbed me when he talked like this. I was always glad when he stopped questioning me and let me go. But he wouldn't leave me alone for long. He tried to get me to tell him what was in every room in Cefn, and where my aunt could possibly have hidden her possessions — her rings and brooches and papers. He kept on telling me that if what I said was true then somebody ought to go and show up Jago for the swindler that he really was. This was what I had always hoped would happen, that I would find someone to take my part against Jago, but I could not help feeling that Tom was less concerned with what I had lost than with what he might get out of it for himself.

There was only one thing he had not wormed out of me — the fact that I still had the will on me. Nobody knew this except myself.

Some time after this he told me that he was going away for a few days. Before he went away, he told me that I was to stay where I was. I was on the point of telling him that he was not my master, but, not for the first time, I held my tongue. Anyhow, I had nowhere to go, and besides I was curious to know what Tom was up to.

Tom and I were not the only ones to have our secrets. It seemed to me that most of the men and women who came to Llanbedr had something to hide. There was one man whom I often watched who was in the habit of taking himself off to some quiet corner of the churchyard. Then, thinking himself hidden behind some headstone or tomb, he would set about going through his clothes, feeling the length of the seams, turning out his pockets and fingering the ragged lapels of his jacket. He was like a treasure seeker going over ground where he thinks something valuable may be hidden. Maybe he had hidden something and forgotten where he had put it. Maybe he had stolen or begged the clothes, and was going through them, hoping that something precious might have been left in them. I never saw him come upon anything, but he spent hours feeling every square inch of his dirty garments, hoping for a lucky find. Once he caught me looking at him, and started away guiltily as if he had been caught stealing, but it was not long before he was back at his old ways.

The church too had its secrets. In my first days at Llanbedr, before I grew lazy, I used to try to tidy it, and would constantly come upon little parcels of mouldy apples, rotting potatoes, ham-bones, stale bread, collections of buttons and pennies and bootlaces that someone had hidden away. Whatever was rotten and smelly I threw away, but the rest I left, because the tramps were like children, always squabbling about their possessions, and didn't like anyone meddling with what they had hidden.

Chapter 16

Hunger

I felt safe as long as I was at Llanbedr, but I was hungry. I had always had a good appetite, but my aunt always fed me well and I never went short. Now, though we always had a great supper whenever Mr Price held a service and doled out his tribute money, and though the tramps, and Tom especially, appeared to get enough somehow to satisfy them, I was left for days in the company of a man who never bothered to provide for himself, far less for me. From time to time he would take a meal, for which he always paid, I was told, with some farmer or shepherd in the parish, but he did not think of taking me with him. I was left to fend for myself, and I did it by poaching.

Everybody at Talybont did a little poaching, though the gamekeepers were very strict. At Cefn there was no need for me to break the law, but at Llanbedr hunger made me desperate. I began by setting snares for rabbits and hares and taking trout, at first by tickling and then by less honourable methods. Mr Price took his share of whatever I brought in and never asked how I had come by it. As far as he was concerned it might have dropped from the sky like manna and Tom and the rest of the tramps were not slow to realise that I could be relied upon to provide something tasty to go into their stew pots. I soon forgot to think about the rights and wrongs of what I was doing. I grew skilful and cunning, and popular. The tramps had always been a bit suspicious of me because I did not join in with them, but my skill as a poacher raised me in their eyes. So I became a persistent and reckless poacher. I began with rabbits and hares and went on to take pheasants and partridges and to tell the truth I enjoyed out-witting the gamekeepers and coming home with my pockets full of game, and grew vain of my reputation. Most of the tramps were good pickers and stealers, but they were not country bred as I was, and knew nothing of what every boy in Talybont was expert at. I became the cunning moonlighter that could always be relied upon to provide something tasty to go with the bread and butter and bacon that Mr Price's money bought.

Then one day, for the first time in my life, I stole.

I had gone up on the moor to set a few snares, but I saw that the gamekeeper was on the prowl, so I got rid of my gear in case he should take it into his head to search me, and wandered over to the far side of the moor to see if I could pick something up there without being caught. I had no luck, but in a little hollow not far from the top of the moor I came upon a party of young ladies and gentlemen who had come up to have a moonlight supper on the hillside. The ladies must have come up on horseback because there were three ponies, all hobbled, feeding near the hollow. The young men were trying to boil a kettle or something like a kettle, but they were making a hash of it. While I was watching, the tripod of sticks, from which they had slung the kettle, burned through and the water poured over the fire. There was a great deal of laughing and screaming and dashing to the rescue, and eventually the kettle boiled, a large white cloth was spread on the turf and they all sat down to eat. I lay down and watched them from the safety of a clump of gorse, wishing that I was sharing the food they seemed to be enjoying so much.

Then one of the young ladies pointed to the moon. There was more screaming and calling out, and they all got up and rushed up the slope of the hill. A shadow had begun to spread across the face of the moon, as if a little bit of it had been clipped out, and I realised why they had chosen this night for their picnic. They had come to see an eclipse of the moon.

A clear-cut shadow was moving almost perceptibly across the uneven face of the moon, not that rough-edged shadow that comes over it when it is waning, but a sharp arc of blackness. At the moment when the last thin crescent vanished an eerie darkness fell over the world — the clump of heather behind which I was hiding, the ridge, the watchers on the brow of the hill — until my eye rested on nothing but the white tablecloth laid out in the hollow.

The darkness seemed to fall not only upon the outward scene but upon my mind as well, as if, with the extinguishing of the light, unnatural thoughts were aroused in me. Under the cover of that sudden darkness I felt an impulse to do what I had never before thought of attempting. It was to take advantage of the secrecy of the night to steal the food that had been so carelessly left behind to tempt me. In my cloak of invisibility I ran forward towards the abandoned tablecloth. I seized one of the big baskets and put my hand in it. I could tell that there were uneaten provisions there. I picked up from the cloth what was left of a pie and a tart, crammed them into the basket, and made off. I knew that I had to make my escape before the shadow of the eclipse moved away from the face of the moon.

It seems strange to me now, looking back, that I had no interest in the eclipse, that I didn't pause somewhere to look at the spectacle that comes rarely enough in a lifetime, but I didn't even look at the moon until, feeling safe from pursuit, I had sat down and devoured most of what I found in the basket. It was only when I had eaten and drunk my fill that I looked up and saw the moon, the last traces of the brown shadow clearing away from her face, looking down with her old serenity.

Chapter 17

I Lose the Will

Little by little, and without my being aware of it, I grew used to the ways of the tramps and ceased to be offended by them. Worse than that, I grew more and more like them, in speech, in looks and in behaviour. I had begun with good intentions of tidying Mr Price's house and getting him to live in a more cleanly way, and to take more pride in his church, but when after a while I found that, far from being grateful for my efforts, he never seemed to notice them, and never knew whether his bed had been made or not, or whether he was drinking from a clean cup or a dirty one, I lost heart. Nor were the tramps any better. Whatever I tidied for them they untidied again in a few minutes. The very day after I had swilled down the floor of the church it would be littered again with crusts and bones. I gave up trying to keep things clean, and began myself to fall into the sluttish ways of my companions. I ceased to care about my own appearance, and neglected to wash or to mend my clothes. Worse than that, I became almost as greedy and grasping as the worst of the tramps. When my shirt grew too dirty, rather than wash it, I would look round for another that someone had carelessly left lying around, and would take it without asking whether it was mine or not. So I let myself sink, until one day I was brought abruptly to my senses.

I was in the church, no longer seeking to make it more decent, but on the lookout for whatever might have been left behind. One of our great pastimes was nosing around to see what could be picked up. I went into the vestry, and saw, hanging on a row of pegs, two or three old surplices, yellow with age and streaked with dirt as if they had been used as towels. I unhooked them, wondering what might be behind them, and found myself looking into a long mirror that was leaning against the wall, the kind of long mirror I had once seen in the vestry at Pentre. I had once seen the parson standing in front of it, looking at himself before he went out to take the service. This was a dirty old mirror. The surface was spotted with stains and the silver backing was beginning to peel off. But it was not the condition of the mirror that shocked me. It was the image that stared back at me as I uncovered it.

I could scarce realise that it was myself I was looking at. My clothes were snagged and torn. My face was dirty, like a sweep's face, with lines of grime on my brow and cheeks. That soldierly bearing I had once tried to put on had given way to an ugly slouch. I realized with a shock that it was not the image of myself that looked back at me, but the picture of Jago. My hair had grown, and had fallen into the position that his hair took — straight and lank and covering the ears. Even the expression on my face seemed to be his — watchful, suspicious, cunning. I had not seen myself clearly for a long time. Mr Price had no looking glass of any kind in his house. And I was filled with dread, as if some strange transformation had come over me, and was still altering my appearance and my nature. I covered the hateful image with the surplices, and stood trembling as if a fever had come upon me.

Bewildered and incredulous, I turned and hurried out of the church, seeking to put as much space as possible between me and the mirror.

Not far from the church the stream that ran down to the Wye broadened and deepened here and there into pools. When I first came to Llanbedr I had been in the habit of washing there and soaking my dirty linen, but that, like most of my good habits, had been given up. Now I made up my mind that before I did anything else that day I would go down to the water and clean off the grime and dirt that I had seen in the mirror. I found a piece of soap and went downstream, as far as I could from the church. Then I stripped, threw my clothes behind a bush and gave myself a good scrubbing. The water was cold but I didn't mind. As I washed the dirt off my hands and legs I felt that I was making a new start for myself.

But my delight in the feeling that I was turning over a new leaf was short-lived. When I came out of the water I found that somebody had quietly and cunningly stolen my belt. The loss of the little money I still had was nothing, but with it had gone my last passport to respectability and safety — the will.

Chapter 18

Marking Time

While Tom was away, I did my best to look after Mr Price. He was if anything more silent and withdrawn than ever, and had apparently completely forgotten his plan to teach me his special shorthand system. He smiled less and there was an anxious look on his face at times. Eventually he told me that he had had some losses and his personal income was so much reduced that he feared he could no longer afford the fees he had been paying out to the tramps for attending his services. The sixpence he had given them for each attendance would have to be reduced to fourpence, and instead of three shillings for a wedding the bonus would be two shillings.

The tramps had taken the news badly, and I was shocked at the way in which they spoke of it.

"It's a flaming disgrace, that's what it is! We've always had sixpence. We're entitled to it."

"If he thinks I'm going to help to keep his church full at fourpence a kick, he's mistaken. I'm goin' to shove off somewhere else."

"He wouldn' have nobody, would he, if we didn't go to his stinking church. Well, he can keep it."

"Bloody old choker: off his nut, anyhow."

"It's just a blab. He has the money all right. He just doesn' want to part wi' it."

"Just wait till Tom comes back. He won't put up wi' this."

It sickened me to hear them talking like this, but to tell the truth this wasn't the only thing that made me feel that the sooner I parted company with them the better. I was now acquainted with the wicked dodges and tricks which they used to impose upon people. There was one man who went out begging every day, but not before he had covered a patch of skin on his leg with soap and then applied vinegar to it so that large mattery blisters seemed to be forming under his skin; and another who used to work red powder into the rims of his eyes — I think it must have been the colouring that Sal used when she wanted to paint Tom — so that they looked sore and inflamed. The two brothers whom I had first seen fishing scraps of food out of their wallet used to practise a shaking and shivering, as if they were about to fall into some kind of fit.

"You has to do things like this," one of them said to me, "or nobody will take no notice of you. You have to look as if you have the shakes, or put on a really bad cough. It's a good lay if you can give yourself out to be blind — a blind dog's a good lay — but my brother and me, we just works the shallow with shaking and shivering."

There was another man who didn't go out begging himself but spent most of his time writing out cards and letters for the others. They called him Sam the Screever, and he used to make out for them cards to hang round their necks telling how they had been crippled fighting for their country or lost their health in distant countries or in taking part in some dangerous expedition. Besides the cards, he would write begging letters for them, in which they presented themselves as survivors of some disastrous shipwreck, victims of some notorious accident, poor deserving workmen whom bad luck or a heartless master had driven on to the roads.

When they found out that I could write, some of the tramps had asked me if I would write out letters and cards for them, and when Sam the Screever got to know, he threatened to knife me if I took his job away from him. He need not have worried. Whatever begging letters I concocted would have been poor affairs, and anyhow I had no intention of setting up in that kind of work.

Now that the summer was coming to an end the tramps were beginning to think of moving into the towns. I caught them from time to time collecting their gear, the men their peas and thimbles, crown and anchor boards, their skittles and biased balls, and their loaded dice, the women with their bottles of fake medicine and beauty lotions. They never spoke openly to me about these things. Although they took whatever I poached for them, they had sensed almost from the beginning that I was not one of them and did not mean to be one of them. When I had refused to become a screever for them they had begun to put even less trust in me. The only one who did not seem to mistrust me was the cheerful feckless Chokey.

How strange it often seemed to me that Mr Price should spend all his days in the company of these liars and deceivers and yet be so saintly. Perhaps it was even more strange and sad that though the tramps spent most of their days in his company, his example meant nothing to them at all, and not one of them was moved by his saintliness and goodness to mend his ways.

Chapter 19

Tom Shows his True Colours

As soon as Tom came back I could see that something had displeased him. He had an ugly and dangerous look on his face. When I had first seen him singing in the Swan I had thought him a fine handsome man. Now that I knew him better, I could see few signs of that handsomeness: his face revealed only greediness, ill-temper, spite. I knew I had better keep out of his way for a while. Something was beginning to tell me that the sooner he and I parted company for good, the better it would be for me.

Shortly after he returned there was a meeting in the church. What they all decided to do about Mr Price's news I did not find out but when Tom came out he looked in an even uglier mood than ever, and it was just at this moment that he ran into Chokey. Poor Chokey, who had not attended the meeting in the church, had taken up his favourite position in the hollow tree just outside the porch, and was back at his game of pretending to be a saint holding up his fingers and making the sign of the cross in the air.

"You bloody lunatic!" shouted Tom. "Didn' I tell you to cut that out? What's the matter with you? Are you deaf as well as daft? Get out of there!"

He pulled Chokey out, holding him with one hand and striking him with the other. As if he knew what was going to happen to him Chokey made no attempt to defend himself, and suddenly Tom seemed to be possessed by uncontrollable fury. He pushed Chokey away and swung his leg viciously at him. At the last moment Chokey flinched and I saw the heavy hob-nailed boot graze his left leg and tear open the leg of his trousers but he was too slow to ward off the second blow. The leg swung again and I heard something crack as the boot struck him just below the kneecap. He toppled forward, and when he was on the ground Tom kicked him again, and I saw blood spread upwards and sideways across his upper cheek. The sight of the blood seemed to incite Tom to greater fury. He kicked and kicked as if he was kicking some animal he had cornered and meant to kill — Chokey's back, his buttocks, his shoulders and even his head.

The attack was so sudden and so unexpected that it was almost over before I knew what was happening. When I did find my voice and tried to interfere, I was seized from behind. Whoever had got hold of me would not let me go. I was flung down and held down. By the time they had let me go, Tom had disappeared and Chokey was lying as still as if he was dead.

Tom came to see me that night. He waited till Mr Price had gone out, and then he came over to the vicarage. I could hardly bear to look at him and he knew it.

"What's up wi' you?"

I didn't answer.

"You saw that Chokey feller playing the fool again, didn' you?"

"Yes, I did."

"Well he did it once too many times. Did you see that knife he flashed at me?"

"He had no knife."

"Oh yes he had. There's lots of things you don't see. He would have got me if I hadn't got him first. Anyhow that's not what I've come to talk about. You know where I've been, don' you?"

"Talybont."

"How did you guess that? Been snooping on me, eh?"

"I have not."

"I been to see that uncle of yours. He's taken over that place of yours, you know. He's quite a favourite in Talybont now."

"But there wasn't anybody who had a good word for him."

"Not now. He's got friends now. You won't be stuck for the price of a drink when Jago's around. But there's some funny rumours going round about you."

"What kind of rumours?"

"They say you've gone to the dogs since you left Taly-bont. In with a parcel of rogues and vagabonds now. And it all started when you ran away wi' your aunt's money."

"What money?"

"The money she had in the house."

"But there wasn' any. I never saw any. I never knew there was any."

"Jago's told them you nobbled it. Your aunt left it to him and ... "

"She didn't!"

"He's got the will to prove it. He's ready to show it to anybody. He showed it to me."

"It's a forgery!"

"How do you know it's a forgery?"

"Because ... "

"Because you've got the proper will, haven' you?"

"No, I haven't."

"You sure?"

"Why should I run away if I have the proper will and it's made out to me?"

"I don't think you're telling me the truth."

"I am."

"I'm beginning to think that your uncle Jago may not be so far wide of the mark after all about you. There's something in your face that tells me that you're lying to me, boy. Well, God help you if I find out, that's all I say."

Before the day ended I went over to find out how Chokey was. The women could be as deceitful and spiteful as the men, but they would help anyone in real trouble. It looked as if Tom's vicious kick had cracked a bone in Chokey's upper shin, but he was not in too much pain.

"I look like Jesus taken down from the cross, don' I, Gareth?" he said.

"Yes, except that you're alive. Why did you pull that knife on Tom?"

"I never had no knife. You didn't see no knife on me, did you?" he asked the women. I was right then. Tom was telling one more lie. I was more convinced than ever that it was foolish to trust anything that he said.

Chapter 20

The Attack

The next day I was working outside the vicarage chopping firewood when one of the tramps came over and said that Tom wanted to see me in the churchyard. I didn't want to go, but I was not yet ready to stand up to him. I put the axe away and walked over to the churchyard.

Tom was sitting smoking on a flat tombstone near the porch. He wasn't alone. In that warm corner where I had seen the women sitting and doing their hair on my first evening at Llanbedr, five or six men were playing cards, and another half a dozen were looking on.

"Come here, Gareth," said Tom, knocking out his pipe and stuffing it away in his coat pocket. "Come here. I got something I want to tell you."

He put his arm inside mine and began to walk me towards the church door. I felt uneasy. There was something determined and vicious about the way he held me, and I tried to disengage myself, but as soon as we got to the door he tightened his grip. Then another arm gripped me on the other side, and a third crooked itself from behind around my neck. I was pushed forward with my head pulled back so that all I could see was the beams across the upper part of the porch and the loose straw of a sparrow's nest. The door was flung open, I was marched up the aisle and then flung violently forward. The sharp edge of the broken chancel step caught my cheekbone and when I put my hand to it I felt the blood running down my cheek. I heard the key turning in the church door, and looked up to see the men ringed round me.

"Come on, now. Hand it over!" said Tom.

"I don't know what you mean."

"Come on, don' come at me with that innocent game!

Give me that paper! The will!"

"I haven't got any will."

"If you don' give it up quietly, we'll get it another way. So make up your mind. Do you give it or do we take it?"

"I haven't got it."

"All right — strip him!"

The men closed in on me. I wanted to hit out at them, but it struck me that the best way of proving to Tom that I was telling the truth was to submit. So I let them strip off coat and shirt, waistcoat, trousers, stockings, boots till I was standing against the broken communion rails without a stitch of clothing on me. I wasn't ashamed of my bare body, but I was ashamed of being made to stand undressed in a church, of desecrating the place, although when I looked sideways I could see a little stone carving of Christ on the cross, stripped for his punishment almost as bare as I was.

I stood there watching the men going through the clothes they had torn from me, turning out the pockets, slitting the lining, and feeling the seams inch by inch. They kept tossing the clothes from one to another, each man making a new search. But they found nothing. Furious at being thwarted, Tom came and got hold of me by the neck and pressed me backwards till I could hear the communion rail cracking beneath me.

"You little swindler! You've hidden it somewhere, haven' you? You've given it to somebody! Where is it?"

"I haven't got it. I haven't got it."

"I'll make you talk!" he shouted, then hit me hard across the side of the face. I toppled over, slipped and felt my head crack on the cold stone floor of the chancel. It was a strange sensation, a sudden blow like the striking of a big clapper on a bell. I thought I heard the bell give out a booming note and then I passed out.

When I came to, the first thing I was conscious of was a drop of blood only a few inches away from my eye. I lay looking at it with a stupid kind of concentration. I could not make out where I was. I could not make out how long I had been lying like this. It was as if some strange interval had occurred in my life, and that something had happened in that interval that I would never be able to recall. This was the first time in my life that I had ever fainted or lost consciousness. I could not realise what had happened and didn't seem to know what to do now that I had recovered. I turned over on one side and found myself looking at a dirty stained glass window, hardly knowing whether the picture it carried was real or imaginary. The upper part of the window had been broken and the hole stuffed with rags, but in the lower part I could see the bare and bloodstained legs of the crucified Christ and at the foot of the cross the soldiers were handing round the clothes they had drawn lots for. For a moment, in my confusion, I thought that it was my clothes they were parting but slowly the circle of my consciousness widened and I knew that my real tormentors had left me. The whole wide blackened church was empty.

I still had no desire to move. I put my head down again on the floor, turning it so that I was not pressing on the sore place, and as I turned over I saw something else only a few feet away from me. It was an old hassock that had been pushed into the hollow under the pew seat. It looked as if the straw had been pulled out and then stuffed back again. I lay looking at it with the same stupid half-comprehending look I had given the blood and the window, but my head cleared once more and I saw something familiar sticking out of the straw. It was the end of my belt. I reached out and pulled it free. It came unwinding like a snake, and as I drew it to me I felt along its length. The money, as I had expected, was gone, but a crackling noise told me that the oilskin was still there. I pulled it. Inside was the will, untouched and as far as I could see untampered with.

I picked myself up and put my clothes on, slowly and clumsily, article by article. When I tried to stand upright, a dizziness swept over me, and I had to put my head down to stop myself from fainting again. I knew I had to get out of the church, so I went forward crouchingly, bent like an old man. Luckily the door was open and the churchyard empty. I managed to get across the field and into the vicarage. Fortunately Mr Price was not at his desk. He was standing under one of the cherry trees in the garden talking to himself. I threw myself on my palliasse, pulled the rough bedding around me, and lay down to wait till life and strength would come back to me.

Chapter 21

A Hope and A Disappointment

I did not stir from the vicarage for the rest of the day, but as soon as it was dark, I got up. I still felt sore, and there was a big swelling on the side of my head, but the rest had done me good and cleared my brain. I was determined to put myself out of Tom's reach. Without disturbing Mr Price — it was easy to deceive him because he never knew where I was going and what I was doing — I made a bundle of some of the bedding, put whatever food I could find into my pockets, and prepared to spend one more night in the open.

When I was far enough away to feel safe, I found myself a shelter, a little clear space in a big clump of gorse and, to tell the truth, I was almost as snug and comfortable there as I had been in the vicarage but I slept only fitfully, and kept waking to see the stars glinting in the dark spaces between the clouds, and the moon, almost full again, and riding high, hard and bright like a lucky stone, dipping for cover as though it was being hunted. As soon as it began to grow light I heard a lark, and saw the hares loping off across the moor. I got up, ate a little, washed my hands and face, and began to consider what to do next.

It was a still day. There were no curlews or greenshanks calling as they did in Spring, no plovers turning and twisting, only two or three buzzards, turning in tiny circles, very high in the air. Somewhere in the north someone was burning heather, and a trail of white smoke dragged slowly across the skyline. Not far from where I was, three blackbirds were swallowing the last berries on a mountain ash. Then I heard a grouse give its alarm call and whirr away over the gorse.

I looked to see what had disturbed it, and saw a man's

head bobbing over the top of the gorse, and ahead of him the tips of a pony's ears. As soon as I saw the deerstalker with its flaps tied back with frayed ribbon I knew that it was Matty.

At first he did not seem to recognise me, and I was afraid that he would go straight past me, but when I had called out to him two or three times, he stopped. He leant down and looked at me disbelievingly.

"Is that you? Gareth boy? God, I wouldn' have recognised you if you hadn't called out like that. You gone as thin as a lat, boy. And what's that bump on the side of your head? Somebody been knocking you about? Where have you been these last two months?"

"I've been here."

"You got a job then?"

"Not really. I've been living with Mr Price, the parson."

"What did you run away from Talybont for?"

"I was frightened."

"Frightened what of?"

"Of Jago. He tried to kill me. He tried to run me down on the Fron. He was mad — like his sister was."

"No, no, Gareth. I can't believe that. I don't know who put this idea into your head, boy, but it's time you were getting rid of it, if you ask me. You've always been on about that uncle of yours. Why didn't you come and see me?"

"You were away at Brecon."

"Then why didn' you tell Richard of Nant Bran or one of the others that Jago was trying to get at you?"

"Because I knew they wouldn't believe me. They were all against me."

"Seems to me you got an idea in your head that everybody's against you. Why shouldn' they believe you?"

"Because of Evan Lloyd."

"That boy that fell in the cesspool?"

"Yes."

"That would have all died down, man, if you hadn't cleared off. You didn't do yourself any good by doing that, did you? You know what they said at Talybont?"

"What?"

"You must have had a guilty conscience to clear off like you did."

"But I wasn't guilty."

"Well, you picked a queer way of proving it, didn' you?"

"I didn't think anybody would side with me. I ran away until I could get somebody to stick up for me and then I would tell everybody the truth."

"What truth?"

"That Cefn was really mine. That Jago just wanted to get rid of me so that he could have it."

"Steady on, Gareth. You'll have a bit of a job making people believe that. Jago says she left it to him. He's been showing everybody your aunt's will. He says he came across it in the house."

"It's not the right will. It must be a forgery."

"How do you know that?"

"Because that's the proper will. That's it. That's the right one. Look at it. You know her writing — my aunt's writing. That's it, isn't it?"

I held out the will to him, and he read it slowly. When he had got right through it, I saw him start again at the top.

"Is this genuine, Gareth?"

"Yes. She gave it to me before she died."

There was another long pause. I had never known Matty take so long to make up his mind about anything.

"Will you keep it for me, Matty?"

"What?"

"It isn't safe here. It's been stolen once. One of the tramps stole it."

"I'll keep it for you — but what do you want me to do with it?"

"Show it to the people of Talybont."

"I can show it to them but it's a pound to a pinch of salt that they won't believe it's genuine. It'll be your word against Jago's, and I don't mind telling you they'll be a sight more ready to believe him than you — especially after what you've done."

"But it isn't just me against him — it's this will against his."

"There's something in that — and this looks genuine

enough to me. We've got a fight on our hands here, Gareth. But I know your poor old aunt won't rest in her grave until everything's put to rights. I'll tell you what to do. You lie low here for a few days till I work out what's best to do. And I'll get a message through to the parson as soon as I want you."

So at last I parted with my will, and I must say that when I saw Matty folding it away in his pocket I felt like Christian in the story when he got near the end of his journey and felt his burden roll away from his back.

I was so relieved to have seen Matty again that I prepared to take his advice without thinking twice about it, but once he had gone and I was left again to my own thoughts and devices it struck me that what he had recommended was more easily said than done. How was I to lie low? I could not return to the vicarage because I could not bear to face Tom again, nor could I continue for ever to live like a beast of the field. It was now September, and though it was dry, the nights were getting cold.

It was at this moment that there came into my mind the memory of the kind shepherd's wife who had given Tom and me food and drink on that day when we were on our way to Llanbedr. The hill farmers of Radnorshire were well-known for their kindness to the poor. At Michaelmas it was the custom for the poor to go round the farms begging for milk, and they were never refused. It was said that the farmers did this in remembrance of the gifts that the shepherds had brought to the infant Jesus at Bethlehem.

Then I remembered too how the shepherd's wife had said that the farm was too big for one man and her husband ought to have some help. I made up my mind that I would go back to the farm and ask the shepherd if he would take me on, even if it was only for a few days.

I have a good memory for places, and I was sure that I could find my way back along the track that Tom and I had taken and there was little fear of getting lost because the weather was clear and open and I could see for miles. Before me rose the great hills of the Forest of Radnor, the dark mass of the Black Mixen and the cone of Whimble topping it. Nothing can describe the relief I felt at turning my back on Llanbedr, on Tom and his crew of hangers-on, and facing once more those lofty free hills.

I made no mistakes, and by midday I was within sight of the farm I was making for. The hills were very quiet. It was the time for silence for the moorland birds, but as I went closer to the house, I could hear the screaming of the house martins flying towards the walls of the farm, then darting away, circling the house and returning to press themselves close to the walls on which they had built their clay nests. I knew what they were doing. They too were getting ready for flight. They were taking a last look at the sheltered places under the eaves to which they meant to return when another Spring came round. They were fixing in their minds the places where they had nested. House martins always build where the air is good, and if they've brought up a brood in a safe place they'll come back to it. I sat watching them, wondering if I would be as safe and happy there as they had been.

My spirits rose as I drew near to the house, and saw the washing spread out on the currant bushes outside the door. I was filled with a longing to be back at work. Perhaps the shepherd would let me help him to harvest the bracken, or thatch his peat stack. I would have been content to take a spade and work in his vegetable garden or muck out the cowhouse — anything so long as I was working. I was tired of the sullen grumbling of the tramps, their jealousies and their tricks, their talk of cheating and stealing and swindling. But I was more tired of idleness. Maybe, if the shepherd would take me on, I would be able to do an honest day's work again, and sit once more at a clean table.

The bad-tempered turkey cock was pecking around by the barn door, but he did not come for me this time, and I took this as a good sign, but the shepherd's wife did not greet me with the kindness she had shown before. She kept scanning my face as if to make sure she was not mistaking me, and when I told her what I had come for, she said she would have to go and ask her husband.

It was some time before he came out to see me, and when he did appear I knew that I had better put out of my mind all hopes of being taken on by him. He was a tall handsome man, as blond as his wife was dark, but I could see that he was displeased.

"Are you the boy that's looking for work?"

"Yes."

"You've been here before, haven't you?"

"Yes. Your wife gave me some milk. I saw you cutting bracken on the hill. She said it was a big farm and that you could do with some help. That's why I've come back."

"You're a cool young fellow, aren't you?"

"Why do you say that?"

"I don't know how you have the nerve to stand there and look me in the face — and ask me for work, as well."

"What do you mean?"

"You know what I mean. What happened to that clutch of eggs you took out of my barn?"

"I don't know."

"You stole them, didn't you?"

"I didn't."

"And now I suppose that big hulking feller has sent you back to see what else you can steal, eh?"

"No. I came of my own accord."

"It's as much as I can do to keep my hands off you, you young blackguard! I want no thieves working for me. So just you turn round, boy, and clear off, and get away from this place as fast as you can!"

"I didn't steal anything."

"Clear off, or else I'll leave my mark on you! I've seen enough of the likes of you, and if ever you come pestering my wife again I'll set the dogs on you!"

I burned with shame as I turned away from him. I could not even begin to explain that I wasn't the thief or even the thief's accomplice. How could I begin to tell to an angry man the full story of Jago and Tom and my aunt and her will? No doubt he had had to listen to many a made-up story such as that. It was not only the loss of my hopes of being taken on that saddened me. It was the loss of my good name. No one had ever called me a thief before. No one had ever humiliated me like this. My cheeks burned when I thought

84

how low I had sunk to be classed among rogues and liars and thieves. I had not minded Jago's insults because I knew there was no substance to his charges but the reproaches of a man whose wife had been kind to me and whose kindness I had abused were not easy to bear.

I lived for the rest of the day on blackberries and whin-berries, some apples that I got from a tree that was still growing in the garden of an abandoned farm, and the remains of the bread and cheese I had brought with me. Then I went back to my hiding place in the gorse, and pulled out the bedding from where I had hidden it. It was dry. It would keep me warm for one more night. The next day I would speak to Mr Price and ask him if he would help me to get away from Llanbedr and Tom for good.

Chapter 22

Tom Makes a Move

I was up early again. It was colder than the first morning I had spent on the moor, and I had to keep the bedclothes huddled around me to keep warm, but being up early had this advantage for me: it enabled me to keep an eye on everything that was happening below me.

As usual it was the women who appeared first. They lit a fire against the wall of the church and began to boil their kettles. Then after breakfast they began to move off. It looked as if it was one of their days for begging or selling. Then just before midday I saw the men coming out of the church and begin to poke around among the food that the women had left for them. When they had finished, they began to pack away what was left into their pockets and wallets, and lace up their boots as if they were preparing for a long walk. When Tom came out, one of the men filled his pipe for him and lit it and handed it to him. They all sat down around him and I could see him gesturing and point-ing as if he was outlining some manoeuvre he had in mind. Eventually they all got up and began to move off. They were all heading in the direction of Talybont.

When they were well out of sight I came out of hiding, ran down the hill and cut across the churchyard, and as I ran past the porch I heard a voice call out to me, "Bless you, my son, bless you!"

I looked round and saw that the voice came from Chokey, ensconced once more in his favourite place, the hollow of the big yew tree. He lifted his fingers and made the sign of the cross over me. He looked thinner and there was a scar on his right cheek. Somebody had patched the tear in his trousers.

"Chokey! What are you doing here? I thought all the men had gone with Tom?"

"Not me. I wouldn' go with him. I kept out of the way."

"Where have they gone?"

"They've gone to get that uncle of yours."

"Jago?"

"I don' know his name. The one that pinched your aunt's place and her money."

"What are they going to do?"

"It's all fixed for tonight."

"What's fixed?"

"They're going to run him out of that house. There's a fortune in there, isn' there? Where neither moth nor rust doth corrupt. Gareth! Don' run away! I want to give you a benediction ..."

I didn't wait to hear any more. I had to see Mr Price and find out what he knew. I found him. He was sitting as usual at his makeshift desk, blocking the way into the house.

"Mr Price! There's going to be a raid on Cefn! Tom's going to raid it. I think they're going to kill Jago. Somebody has to warn him."

He did not reply to me but bent down to pick up a scrap of paper that had fallen to the ground. He kept looking at it as if there was something extraordinary written on it.

"Mr Price," I said, "if there's a fight, Jago will be killed. I know what Tom's like. He thinks there's money in the house, and he'll do anything for money. If there's a fight, Jago will get killed."

Again he did not reply. He kept on looking at the sheet of paper in his hand, then pulled a face as if there was something in it that offended him.

"Read that," he said, passing it to me.

"I can't. I don't want to. I don't want to talk about your silly shorthand. I'm talking about my uncle. And my house."

"Sometimes," he said, "I don't find it very easy myself. Now what does this part say?"

For the first time I lost my temper with him. Why was he not listening to me? Was his brain beginning to go? Or was he playing some kind of game with me, pretending not to

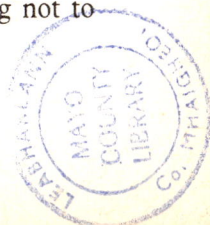

87

understand so that he would not have to answer my question, so that he would not have to confess to himself that these men he had befriended were violent and dangerous criminals?

"You're mad!" I shouted. "You'll stand by and let them do anything so long as you're left in peace to waste your time in stupid things like that shorthand. If Jago's murdered, the blame will be partly yours."

Then I ran out and started for Talybont. I did not know what I was going to do, but I knew I had to get to Jago before Tom did.

For the first time I began to be troubled with the suspicion that I was the one who had set in motion these violent actions. I began to ask myself if I had been just to Jago. Had I been too ready to think the worst of him — as the people of Talybont had been too ready to think the worst of me? I had made him out to Tom and to Matty to be a dangerous lunatic, a thief, and a would-be murderer. Yet to many he had been looked upon as a kind brother, and a good neighbour, and one who had as much right to my aunt's possessions as I had. He had laid violent hands on me and he had told lies — but he was not the only violent and untruthful man in my world and I was not altogether honest and guiltless myself. Now he was in danger from the mob of layabouts and vagabonds at whose hands I had myself suffered, and if I did not lift a finger to help him I would be as big a scoundrel as I had made him out to be. Hateful though he was to me, I knew that if I did not try to warn him I would regret it and be sorry for it for the rest of my life.

Chapter 23

The Raid on Cefn

I did not know how far it was to Talybont, but I knew that if it was not beyond the reach of the tramps, it was within mine. I had watched them set off and knew what general direction to take. I knew that I would have to go cautiously because I hadn't the time to make mistakes but I would have been a great fool if I had lost my way, because at every mile or so they had carelessly left some trace or other — an empty bottle, an apple core, a crust, the broken bowl of a clay pipe. Besides, wherever the ground was damp I could see the imprints of their heavy boots.

It was very late in the afternoon when I caught up with them. They had settled down in a little hollow which I judged to be about two miles outside the village. They were apparently waiting for the darkness to fall before beginning their attack, and I looked round for a vantage point from which I could keep an eye on them without being observed. I found the perfect place behind two rocky outcrops that stood so close together that they made a narrow slit, like the space in a castle wall through which archers used to shoot, narrow enough for me to hide but wide enough to see what every man was doing. They had all thrown themselves down on the turf and were drinking, passing bottles and cans around. There were sixteen of them, but some had already drunk too much and were sitting with their heads between their knees. Only Tom seemed to be in command of himself. He sat upright, alert and aggressive, drinking but spitting out most of what was offered to him, and puffing on his short clay pipe.

Then, behind them and beyond them, I saw the far horizon begin to glow. A flame-like light caught the lower edge of one long low cloud, and the orange rim of the moon appeared above the line of mountain on the far side of the valley. Inch by inch, with a serene and stealthy motion, it grew and filled, and then like a great golden balloon it lifted itself clear of the rim of the mountain, and floated upwards, cooling and paling as it rose, hardening from orange to gold, from gold to primrose, from primrose to silver, as if it knew what scene of violence and bloodshed it might be called upon to witness, and was blanching at the prospect.

Tom had timed his attack well. In half an hour it would be dark enough for the attackers to hide, but light enough for them to do whatever deed of destruction they were bent upon.

Turning to the west I saw the sun go down as the moon rose. The fiery confused colours of its setting were flung upwards and outwards like the fires of a great explosion. The sun was floundering, and the ragged clouds closed over it as it sank.

As soon as it had vanished I moved cautiously out of my hiding place and made for Cefn. I was not quite sure of my purpose and plan, but I knew that I had to get there before Tom did. But before I came to the edge of the village I saw someone walking towards me — a thin man, with a wide tattered hat on his head. It was Mr Price, and he was following a path lower down the hill, a way that would keep him clear of Tom and his men. What was he doing here? How had he managed to outstrip us all? I thought for a moment of running down to him and asking him why he was here but I was afraid to waste time. Would he understand what was going to happen? Would he hold me up while I tried to get an answer from him? I let him go and went on.

As soon as I came to Cefn I knew what he had been doing. The door was shut fast. There was no smoke coming from the chimney. The house was empty and deserted. Someone, I was sure, had warned Jago that the men were after him, and he had fled. Even the cowhouse was padlocked. Nobody in Talybont locked his stock up unless some serious trouble was brewing. I went round the house trying every door and window. They were all locked. I had just finished when I heard the attack begin.

And then I had to stand by and watch a demented onslaught on the house that had once been my home. Enraged at finding it empty and locked against them, the gang began on the windows, smashing them with sticks and stones. Then the doors were broken in, and from my hiding place behind that very wall which had sheltered Jago I heard the furniture being shattered, the cupboard doors being ripped off, the pans and kettles banging and clattering on the stone floors.

How they discovered where Jago had gone, and what mad fit drove them to go after him I never properly knew. I saw no one in Talybont come near them. On the contrary, the villagers, as if they had all taken fright, or had been too much taken by surprise to join forces, had all taken refuge behind closed doors. Everywhere I could hear doors being slammed, bolts being shot home and women crying out in alarm, and see lights going out. But someone must have informed against Jago or been forced to give him away. The men rushed through the village kicking doors, smashing the windows, and trying to force a way into the Swan. Then they headed for the Fron. It seemed madness to me to think that a man could be run to earth on a moor even in moonlight as strong as this but someone who knew where Jago was to be found must have been leading the chase and the men themselves seemed to have taken leave of their senses. Some said later that it was Tom who had urged them on this disastrous chase. They'd heard him shouting that Jago had taken the money with him and they'd never get a penny till they had laid hands on him. There was probably more to it than that. They had been drinking from the moment they set out. They were spoiling for a fight even before they got to Cefn. They must have lost their heads when they found that they had worked themselves up to attack a man that wasn't there and lay their hands on a fortune that nobody could find. Now they were ready to do anything, however stupid and unreasonable it was, to vent their rage and spite.

Then I heard someone cry out, and for the first time saw that they had not been misinformed. Jago was there, in front of us, seeking refuge among the rocks through which he had hunted me not long ago. Like me he was running into a trap of his own making.

I watched him running like a fox, twisting in and out of the gorse and furze and scrambling over the hard moonlit rocks. From time to time he tried to double back, but on every occasion he was seen and headed back. Then he seemed to give up all hope of breaking through the line of his pursuers or of throwing them off the scent and I realised that he was making for the waterfall, as if he remembered the day when he was the hunter and I the quarry, and I had eluded him by daring to jump the fall.

"He's making for Break Its Neck!" somebody shouted, and the long drawn-out line of the hunters drew together. We were just in time to see him slithering down the first drop, drawing himself up on the lip of the rapid and looking despairingly behind him. Then he slid down the second drop, staggered a little as if he was losing his footing, regained his balance, then flung himself out into the air like a crow taking flight. I saw his thick arms outspread like black wings, and the ragged ends of his coat splayed like black feathers. He didn't jump feet foremost as I had done, but flung himself clumsily into the air. We heard the splash as he hit the pool, then all other sounds were swallowed again in the roar of the waterfall.

I heard somebody splash across the stream above the fall, jumping from stone to stone and floundering in the water. He got across and I heard him shout that he could see somebody moving about down below. As soon as he called out the men began to fan out on both sides of the ravine. I wanted to shout and tell them to be careful, and that the slopes were treacherous, but I did not want to give myself away. I heard somebody shouting for help as he lost his footing and fell, crashing into trees and saplings as he slid towards the water.

From then on all question of pursuing Jago was forgotten. All the men's energies were concentrated on getting out of danger and escaping from this dark ravine that seemed to wish to engulf them and suck them down into its dangerous depths. When they could see that the insane impulse to hunt and to kill had left them, they all began to troop back to Talybont.

This time they were not to have everything their own way. As they came close to the village they saw the men of Talybont waiting for them. Now they were armed. In every hand there was a pitchfork, a sickle, a flail, a club. I saw the moonlight glint on the barrel of a rook rifle as it was raised. Then a warning shot was fired into the air. This was enough for Tom's men. They scattered without a fight and vanished in the folds and hollows of the hill.

The attack on Cefn was over. The attackers had fled across the moor, and showed no signs of returning. The defenders walked back to their homes, and one by one the lights went out. Nobody noticed me as I worked my way back to Cefn and went in. Hardly knowing what I was doing and why I was doing it, I went into the room that had been mine, righted the overturned bed, lifted the slashed mattress back on it, and fell asleep.

The last thing I remembered was that I recognised the man who had fired the rook rifle. It was Matty, but how he had come to be in Talybont was more than I could explain.

Chapter 24

After the Raid

I was wakened by Matty shaking my shoulder.

"What are you doing here, boy? Somebody said you'd been seen, but I didn' believe them. You'd better get moving out of this place afore you get into trouble."

"But this is my house!"

"It's not the house I'm talking about. It's what happened last night."

"I didn't do anything."

"Who's going to believe that? That mob smashed windows and kicked in doors. And you were with them. You were seen."

"I wasn't with them, Matty. I was trying to warn Jago."

"They'll never believe you, Gareth. The best thing for you is to clear off for a few days."

"But I don't want to clear off. This is my house and now that Jago's gone I want to come back and live here."

"There'll be a bit of clearing up to do before they'll take you back. There's been some queer stories going around in Talybont about you."

"Mr Price will back me up."

"That daft old parson?"

"Yes. He knows I came back to warn Jago."

"Then I think I'd better go and fetch him. Tell you what, Gareth. Just you lie low here till I bring him back here. I'll get Mrs Priddy to let me have the trap. But don't you show yourself, boy, or else you might get yourself torn to pieces."

For the rest of the day I didn't stir out of Cefn. There was one cupboard where I could hide and which I could fasten from the inside. Whenever I heard anyone coming I retreated there. It was a strange thing to sit hidden there and listen to the comments of the men and women who came to see the damage that Tom and his men had done, and to learn what they thought of my aunt and Jago and the tramps and me.

"Poor old Susannah! — Isn't it a good job now that she's dead and gone? It would have broken her heart to see what they have done to her comfy little house."

"That Jago had it like a pigsty, mind."

"It was a bad thing for Cefn when that nephew of hers had to give it up."

"Yes, but they say he's gone to the bad, and he's worse than Jago now. He was with that mob that did all the damage here last night."

"I suppose he did it to get his own back on Jago."

"But look at all the damage they done! They've slit all the cushions and broken all the pictures."

"And they pulled up the floorboards, as well. It will take Jago some time to put this right when he comes back."

"If he comes back. You know where he went last night. My husband says he went over Break Its Neck and it isn't many that comes back once they been over there."

"Poor Jago. My husband says he wasn' such a bad feller, after all was said about him."

"But I always said there was something fishy about him. I always said that Susannah must have been out of her mind to leave Cefn to him. Because she couldn' abide him, could she?"

"And what will happen to the place then if Jago doesn't come back?"

"It will just go to rack and ruin, I suppose, like that place at Risca where they used to have the dances. The quarterly dances, remember, Eirlys? You wouldn' recognise the place now. I used to think that Susannah was a very lady-like woman, but her relations haven't turned out very grand, have they?"

I longed to be able to burst open the door and say, "No. You are wrong. You are all wrong. I haven't gone to the bad. I'm here and Cefn is mine now and I am going to look after it so that it doesn't go to rack and ruin!" I was sick and weary of always hiding. Ever since Jago had driven me away from Talybont I seemed to have lived like a hunted animal, hiding in my cave, hiding on the Fron, hiding away from Tom and his men on the Llanbedr moors, hiding now in a cupboard in my own house. I longed to be done with secrecy and deceit and flight and hatred. If only I could go out on to the Fron again, like a free man, and look after my flock, and be afraid of nothing and be suspected of nothing! But I did not even dare to fling open the cupboard door and say, "I am here and am innocent and this is my rightful home!" Instead I had to sit and suffocate in the musty darkness of a dirty cupboard and wait and pray that in the end my name would be cleared.

It was late when Matty came for me.

"I've got Mr Price with me," he said. "We've got a bit of a fight on our hands, but if Mr Price comes up trumps we'll pull through. Half the time he doesn't know where he is, does he? The men are all in Mrs Priddy's waiting for us."

Chapter 25

My Name is Cleared

Although I had spent many a night looking through Mrs Priddy's window, I had never been in the Swan. I was surprised to find it was quite homely inside, like a big farm kitchen with a trestle table with three barrels draped with wet cloths, benches, settle and spittoons, and a big fireplace with a glass case over the mantel and a stuffed pike in it. Most of the men looked up at us when we went in, and kept looking in an unfriendly way, but there were two strangers who did not seem to know or to care about what was going to happen and turned straight back to their game of dominoes. Mrs Priddy hurried forward as we went in, but when she saw Mr Price she looked a bit put out, and didn't drop a curtsey to him as I'd seen her doing to other parsons. I think she was taken aback to find that the clergyman she had been expecting was no more than a skinny old man in an old cassock and muddy boots. Nobody greeted us except a dog that got up from the hearth and came over to smell us, but a word from someone sent it back to its place by the fire with its tail between its legs. Matty ordered cider for us and for a few moments we drank in silence. The only sounds in the room were the ponderous ticking of the grandfather clock and the clicking of the dominoes in the corner. Mr Price sat drinking his cider as if it had been nectar.

"We'd better get down to a bit of plain speaking," said Matty. "There's a lot of things here that's got to be cleared up. I'm not a Talybont man ..."

"We know that," said a voice from the back.

"But you all know me, and you've all worked with me, and I'm going to take the liberty of telling you that you've all let yourselves be badly taken in these last few weeks."

97

"Nobody took us in!"

"Oh yes, they did, and I'll come straight to the point: Jago Pritchard did for one!"

"Jago was all right to us!"

"He wasn' frightened to come here. And he wasn't frightened to put his hand in his pocket, either."

"He had plenty of money," said Matty, "but where did he get it from? He bought drinks for you because he wanted to keep you quiet — but where did it come from? I'll tell you. He pinched it."

"That wasn' his story, Matty. If anybody had done any stealing and pinching it was Gareth Pritchard."

"He pinched the money that should ha' come to Jago."

"Now, listen, and for God's sake use your heads. Do you think a young man with money in his pocket would go and live in a place like Llanbedr with tramps and rogues? He wouldn' have kept it long in a place like that. And look at him. Does he look like somebody that's been living on the fat of the land?"

"We didn' say that. We said he took Jago's money."

"You got it all the wrong way round. Jago was the thief. He stole Cefn, the flock, the Fron, the lot."

"It was left to him."

"He had a will to prove it."

"Oh yes, the will. Well I'm going to give you a surprise over that. But just you wait. There's something else."

"By God, there is," shouted a tall man, jumping up angrily. "What about what happened here last night? What about that gang he brought over here, smashing windows and frightening the life out of the women and the children? What about that? Who's goin' to pay for all that damage?"

Matty paused for a moment before replying. Then he turned to Mr Price and said, "This is your cue, sir. Let's hear your side of the story."

Mr Price had not uttered a word up to this point. He had stopped smiling and looked as if he had not taken in a single word and my heart sank as I saw that puzzling absent look come over him. Was he going off in to one of those maddening fits of absent-mindedness in which no one could get any sense out of him? When he began "My friends, my neighbours, there was a man whose name was Stephen ..." I saw one of the Talybont men tap his forehead as if to say, 'the old man's off his nut again', and Matty looked uneasy. "Stephen testified on his Saviour's behalf," went on Mr Price. "And the more he testified the more the wicked raged against him. And they stoned him, and when they stoned him he lifted up his voice and said, 'Father forgive them for they know not what they do.'"

"What's Stephen got to do wi' us, parson?" said the tall man. "We don' want to hear about him."

"We don' want no sermons!"

"It is not a sermon," cried Mr Price, "and Stephen has everything to do with the case in hand. Wait till I come to the end and then judge for yourselves."

I looked up in surprise. I had never heard him speak so clearly. After all he *had* heard what the men had said, and he knew what he was going to say to them. When the men heard this new note in his voice they stopped their smirking and winking and began to listen attentively to him. "You too," he went on, "have a Stephen among you. I call this boy by that name because he forgave — and he did his best to save (pray to God that he has succeeded) — the very man who had done most wrong to him. Do you know why Jago Pritchard escaped from the hands of those men who meant to do him harm? Because this boy came to me and said that he could not stand by and let his uncle be hunted down. How can you think of rejecting him? He was not one of that band that came breaking your windows and frightening your children. He did not come here with that motive. He came to be the saviour of the man who had done him most harm."

"You may be right, parson, and if we've judged him wrong we're very sorry," said one man.

"But there's something else you've got wrong," said Matty jumping up again. "You said that Jago had a will."

"He had."

"Did he ever show it to you?"

"Many a time. He showed it to all of us, here, in Mrs Priddy's."

"Was it signed?"

"It had Susannah's cross on it."

"But Susannah Phillips was a woman who could read and write. Why should she put a mark when she could write as well as anybody? I'll tell you why. That will Jago showed you was a forgery."

"How do you know that?"

"Because this is the real will! Look at that! Pass it round. Is there a cross there?"

"No, it's a proper signature."

"Which of you can read?"

"I can," said the tall man.

"Give it to him. Is that will properly signed?"

"Yes."

"Is it properly witnessed?"

"Yes."

"And what does it say?"

"It says that everything is to go to Gareth Pritchard my loving nephew."

"There you are then," said Matty. "Why should this boy want to destroy something he knew was his? Why should he want to make enemies of the people he wanted more than anything else to come back to? He's the rightful heir to Cefn — and nobody knows that better than Jago Pritchard. And if I'm not mistaken he'll never set foot in Talybont again."

"I give you back to him," said Mr Price, "like the Prodigal Son. We may not have the fatted calf to kill, but though I look like a pauper, my pocket is not empty. I invite you all to celebrate this happy event. For that which was lost is found again."

I do not know how that Celebration ended, but I know that it ended without Mr Price, who quietly slipped out and, disdaining the trap that had been provided for him walked all the way through the darkness to his cold and lonely hovel in Llanbedr.

I never saw Jago again. There was a rumour that he had been seen in Liverpool, and a man from Builth who had gone to America said in a letter to his brother that there was another man from Radnorshire on the boat he went over in, but he hadn't met him. I thought first that Jago must have found some money in the house, the money that Tom had been looking for, but maybe he paid for his passage with what he got for the sheep he sold. I never knew the real truth about Jago. I hoped that he had gone to America and, though I was sorry that in the end he had to run away from Talybont, I never wanted him back. Nor did I ever want to see Tom Hard-up again, and lived for years in fear of seeing his huge form coming up the land towards Cefn.

Chapter 26

The Will

It was late when I got back to Cefn, but before I went to bed, I lit all the candles I could find and went from room to room, counting up the damage that had been done. It was a sad scene. The mattresses and pillows had all been slashed and the floor was deep in feathers. All the mats had been taken up, and the drawers pulled out and the contents scattered. The seats of the chairs had been ripped open, the pictures torn from the walls, the curtains pulled down from the rails, and everything that could be broken — lamps, china, mirrors, vases, and pictures — had been smashed. Even the floorboards had been prised up, and skirting boards pulled from the walls.

It had never occurred to me to ask myself seriously if my aunt was likely to have hidden any money in the house. I had known next to nothing about her intentions apart from what she had said to me. In fact, difficult though it is to believe, although I had had the will so long, I had never even read it through. I took it out and went carefully through it.

What it said was not surprising — or rather the surprising element in it was neither unexpected nor puzzling. This is what it said.

I, Susannah Phillips, being in my right senses, do hereby give and bequeath all that I possess, namely my house, Cefn of Talybont, and everything in it and belonging to it — my flock of Beulah sheep, my grazing rights on the Fron, and all the money I leave behind me, to my loving great nephew Gareth Pritchard, who has so kindly looked after me and my farm since the death of my husband. What I am now going to add to this last will and testament may sound odd but I think my great-nephew will understand it. I have a sum of money which I wish to hand over to him to use till the time comes when he sells whatever lambs and ewes he wishes to take to market. I am very anxious that this money shall not be stolen from him, so I have left it in the care of a certain Llewellyn in a place where my heir will know to look. This may seem a strange thing to do, but I have not done it without a great deal of thought. I have made my will in this way out of my gratitude to Gareth Pritchard for his loving kindness to me.

Signed

Susannah Phillips

At last I knew why it was that neither Jago nor Tom had been able to find the money my aunt had left behind her. How she had thought of my cave, and how she had managed to find her way there and hide her money without my knowing I could not understand, but Llewellyn had kept her secret: I found the bag of sovereigns in a little recess in the far wall. No one had touched them since they had been hidden there. All the time I had lain shivering in the cave this treasure had been within reaching distance and I had never known of it.

As soon as I could, I went over to Llanbedr to see Mr Price. It was a long walk, but even had it been twice the length I would have undertaken it.

It was late afternoon when I stopped once more on the ridge where on that fateful day in early summer I halted with Tom and first looked down on the little mouse-coloured church. Nothing seemed to have changed. I could see the tower roof, with gaps where the lead had been stolen, the gaps where slates had been blown off the roof of the nave, the churchyard with its tilting tombstones and old yews falling apart from age and neglect, even the scattered groups of tramps waiting for the bell to summon them to service. One or two of the men who had taken part in the raid were there, but Tom was missing. He had been named as the leader of the mob that raided Talybont and a warrant had gone out for his arrest. As far as we knew he was still at large. Nor for that matter was anything known about Jago either.

I had no desire to meet the tramps at closer quarters, even though I could see that Chokey was still one of them, and still acting out his strange game. I walked straight towards the vicarage.

As I had hoped, Mr Price was in. He was sitting at that tottering inky box he called his desk, with his back to the dark, boarded-up rooms. He was reading or praying, maybe preparing himself for the service to come. He seemed to be caught up again in one of those fits of absent-minded meditation that came over him from time to time. I stood still till I felt his spirit coming back to earth again.

"How are you, Mr Price, sir?"

"Very well . . . yes, very well."

"I'm Gareth, Mr Price."

"Oh yes, Gareth."

"I've come to thank you for what you did for me."

"Yes. Yes."

He spoke as if he didn't know what I was referring to and there was an awkward silence.

"I see you are getting ready for your service."

"Yes. I still have my flock. Did you think I would close my church against them?"

"No, but I thought that after . . . after that affair . . . at Talybont they might have been ashamed to come."

"No. No. They know me. I ask no questions. Why should I be less forgiving than you? Didn't I see you forgiving your uncle who had tried to rob you?"

I was about to tell him that I might have saved Jago's life, but I had never forgiven him, and would never forgive him, but at that moment the church-bell began to sound. He got up and began to get ready. I fastened up his dirty old cassock for him, threading the old bootlaces with which he kept it fastened at the back. He did not say goodbye. Perhaps he thought I was going to follow him and take part in the service.

I didn't. I looked through one of the broken windows and saw him standing at the lectern. The place looked more like a thieves' den than ever, the ragged figures sprawling over the ruined pews, the floor littered with rubbish, the dirty walls scrawled over with offensive messages. Of all this squalor Mr Price was, as always, totally unaware. He lifted his eyes from his book and began to recite his familiar lesson.

"A certain man made a feast . . . "

I turned away and began on the long walk back to Talybont.

I knew that I had a huge task before me. It would take me months to make good all the damage that had been done to Cefn, but first of all I wanted to get up on my beloved Fron again. The flock had gone — Jago had sold it — but the grazing was still mine.

On the way I stopped to look at my tree. I still looked upon it as a kind of talisman, although the fortunes it had brought me were as double-natured as its appearance. It had gone. Someone must have felled it and taken it away for firewood. I could not help feeling that this was a good omen. Perhaps Jago and Tom had also gone out of my life for ever.

I was wandering round the empty sheep-walk when Richard of Nant Bran came upon me. I was surprised to see him, especially without his dog. I was even more surprised when he told me he had come over specially to see me. He held out his hand to me and grasped it warmly.

"There's two things I have come over to say to you, Gareth. We had the wrong idea about you. And I've come to make it up with you. I want you to have your dog back, because I can see now that he was sold to me under false pretences."

"Have you got Bryn?"

"Yes. Jago sold him to me, but you can have him whenever you want him."

"I'll pay you for him, Richard."

"No indeed you won't. I'll take nothing. He belongs to you and you'll want him."

"I haven't any sheep now."

"You'll get some. I've made up my mind to give you a start, Gareth, and I know the others will kick in with me. We'll start you up again, boy, never you fear."

In all the happiness that came to me in the next few weeks there was one disappointment and I should have been prepared for it. Bryn seemed to recognise me, but having two masters puzzled him. He had got used to Richard and he couldn't understand me as he used to. He was very obedient and a good worker, but he had changed his ways once and couldn't change again. So in the end I gave him back to Richard and got myself a new dog, a young one, and trained him myself from scratch. I missed Bryn at first, but as soon as I saw how happy he was with Richard I knew I had done the right thing. I called my new dog Llewellyn, and he turned out to be a great working dog, as faithful and clever even as Bryn.